Contents

KT-118-668

QUICK COURSE®

in

ACCESS 97

Computer training books for busy people

JOYCE COX

NATHAN DUDLEY

PUBLISHED BY
Online Press
15442 Bel-Red Road
Redmond, WA 98052
Phone: (425) 885-1441, (800) 854-3344
Fax: (425) 881-1642
E-mail: quickcourse@otsiweb.com
Web site: www.quickcourse.com

Online Press is an imprint of Online Training Solutions, Inc.

Publisher's Cataloging in Publication
(Prepared by Quality Books Inc.)

Cox, Joyce.
    Quick Course in Access 97 / Joyce Cox, Nathan Dudley.
    p. cm.
    Includes index.
    LCCN: 97-66247
    ISBN: 1-879399-73-3

    1. Microsoft Access. 2. Database management.   I. Dudley,
Nathan.   II. Title.

QA76.9.D3C69 1997   005.75'65
                             QBI97-40296

Printed and bound in the United States of America

2-3-4-5-6-7-8-9-A-C-S-S-3-2-1-0

ONE

PART

LEARNING THE BASICS

In Part One, we cover basic techniques for working with Microsoft Access. After you have completed these three chapters, you will know enough to be able to handle the majority of databases you will create with Access. In Chapter 1, you learn how to work with the program while creating a simple database table. In Chapter 2, you customize the table's structure and use forms to enter and view data. Finally, in Chapter 3, you learn how to extract useful information from your databases by using queries and reports.

1

Creating Simple
Database Tables

*Let Access generate
a sequential number
as the primary key*

*Size columns to see
complete entries*

Customers   6/2/97

Customer ID	First Name	Last Name	Address	City	State	Postal Code	Phone Number
1	Jock	Nicholson	123 Joker Street	Hollywood	CA	11403-	(213) 555-1111
2	Laura	Baccall	1171 Whistle Heights	Hollywood	CA	11403-	(213) 555-9297
3	Mel	Gibsand	5941 Warrior Road	Hollywood	CA	11403-	(213) 555-0909
5	Judy	Foster	5454 Silencio Avenue	Hollywood	CA	11403-	(213) 555-6819

Page 1

*To sort this column in
ascending order, click a
button on the toolbar*

*Print in portrait or
landscape mode,
depending on your data*

Other ways of starting Access

Instead of starting Access from the Start menu, you can create a shortcut icon for Access on your Windows 95 desktop. Right-click an open area of the desktop and choose New and then Shortcut from the object menu. In the Create Shortcut dialog box, click the Browse button and navigate to the folder where the Access.exe program is stored (probably Program Files\Microsoft Office). Select the program, click Open, and then click Next. Type a name for the shortcut icon and click Finish. Double-click the icon to start Access. (To delete a shortcut icon, drag it to the Recycle Bin.) For maximum efficiency, you can start Access and open an existing database by choosing Documents from the Start menu and then choosing the database from the Documents submenu, where Windows 95 stores the names of up to 15 of the most recently opened files. If you are using Microsoft Office and have installed the Office shortcut bar, you can click the Open Office Document button on that shortcut bar and navigate to the folder in which the database you want to open is stored, or you can choose Open Office Document from the top of the Start menu. To start Access and open a new database, click the New Office Document button found on the Office shortcut bar or choose New Office Document from the top of the Start menu, and then double-click the Blank Database icon.

You have probably just started to work with Microsoft Access 97 and are excited but nervous about learning to use this powerful database tool. You are hoping that, like other Windows applications, Access will be simple to use and yet offer you the power you need to handle complex data. Well, relax. By the end of this chapter, you'll know how to create database tables, enter data, and move around within the program. If you have used other database applications, a quick review of this chapter will get you going.

Throughout this book, we focus on how to use Access to carry out common database tasks, and for our examples, we show you how to create a database for a small video store. You will easily be able to adapt these examples to your particular needs. Because good database design is essential if you want to take maximum advantage of Access, we have dedicated Chapter 4 to this topic.

We assume that you have already installed both Windows 95 and Access 97 on your computer. We also assume that you've worked with Windows 95 before and that you know how to start programs, move windows, choose commands from menus, highlight text, and so on. If you are a new Windows 95 user, we suggest you take a look at *Quick Course® in Windows 95*, another book in our series, which will help you quickly come up to speed.

To follow the instructions in this book, you must use a mouse. You can perform many Access functions using the keyboard, but a mouse is required for some tasks. You will find the menus and buttons intuitive and easy to use, and in no time at all, pointing and clicking your way around Access will seem perfectly natural.

It's time to get started, so let's fire up Access 97:

1. Click the Start button and choose Programs, and then choose Microsoft Access from the Programs submenu. After a few seconds, you see a window similar to the one shown on the facing page, which asks whether you want to create a new

database or open an existing one. (If the Office Assistant appears first, click the Start Using Microsoft Access option. We'll discuss the Office Assistant more on page 26.)

2. Click the Blank Database option and click OK.

3. When Access displays the File New Database dialog box, click Cancel to close the dialog box so that you can examine an empty Microsoft Access window like this one:

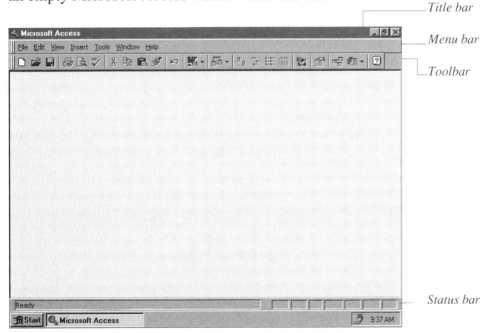

Like most Windows applications, the Access window has a title bar, a menu bar, and a toolbar at the top, and a status bar at the bottom. Let's take a quick look at each of them.

The title bar identifies the program. At its left end is the Control menu (represented by the key icon), which provides commands for manipulating the application's window. At its right end are the Minimize button (the underline dash), which shrinks the application window to a button on the Windows 95 taskbar; the Restore button (the overlapping window frames), which decreases the size of the application window so that we can see other open applications; and the Close button, which exits the program. (If you are running Access as part of Microsoft Office, you may also see the Office shortcut bar.)

The menu bar changes to reflect the menus and commands available for the database component we are working with. The Access menus work the same as those of other Windows applications. To choose a command from a menu, first click the name of the menu in the menu bar. When the menu drops down, click the name of the command you want. To close a menu without choosing a command, click anywhere outside the menu.

Unavailable commands

On the menus, some command names are displayed in gray letters, indicating that we can't choose those commands at this time, and some command names have an arrowhead next to them, indicating that choosing the command will display a submenu. We choose a submenu command the same way we choose a regular command.

Submenus

Dialog boxes

Some command names are followed by an ellipsis (...), indicating that we must supply more information in a dialog box before Access can carry out the command. We sometimes give the necessary information by typing in an edit box. At other times, we might select items in list boxes or click check boxes or option buttons to indicate our selections. We'll use many types of dialog boxes as we work our way through this book, and you'll see how easy they are to work with.

Object menus

Object menus group together the commands used most frequently with a specific type of object, such as a database field or a window element. You display an object menu by pointing to the object and clicking the right mouse button. You can then choose a command from the menu in the usual way.

The toolbar is a row of buttons that quickly access the most commonly used menu commands. Access displays different toolbars depending on the database component we are working with. Currently, we see the Database toolbar with all but three buttons dimmed to indicate that they are unavailable. To avoid confusion, a feature called *ToolTips* helps us determine the functions of each button. When we point to a button, a pop-up box appears with the button's name.

The status bar at the bottom of the Access window displays messages and provides helpful information.

Now that you're familiar with the window's general layout, let's discuss the concept of a database.

What Is a Database?

A database is a structured collection of data items. Because the data's arrangement is predictable, we can manipulate the items to extract useful information. The most basic component of an Access database is a *table* in which information is arranged in *rows* and *columns*. In addition to tables, an Access database can include queries, forms, reports, and other components, all of which allow us to view and manipulate our database information in a variety of ways. As we progress through this book, we will introduce each of these components.

Database components

In this chapter, we'll create a table to hold information about a video store's customers. But before we create our first table, let's take a look at an example that came with Access. The table we will open was created by Microsoft as part of a database for a fictional company called Northwind Traders. To open the Northwind database, follow these steps:

The Open Database button

1. Click the Open Database button on the toolbar. Access displays this dialog box:

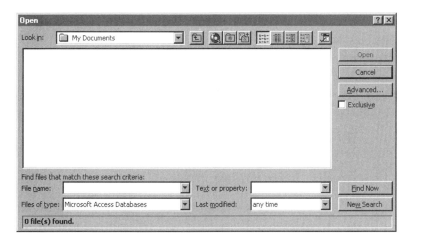

Opening options

The buttons on the toolbar in the Open dialog box allow you to search for files on the Internet or an intranet, work with files in a Favorites folder, and display different levels of detail for each file. You can use the edit boxes at the bottom of the dialog box, the Commands/Settings button, and the Advanced button to find specific files in various ways. (We discuss the Exclusive option on page 152.)

2. Move to the Program Files\Microsoft Office\Office\Samples subfolder, double-click Northwind, and if a window introducing Northwind Traders appears, click OK. Access then displays a database window like this one:

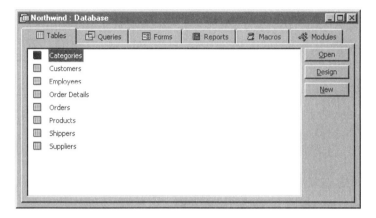

The components of the Northwind database are arranged in categories on tabs in the database window. If the Tables tab is not active, click the tab to display the tables shown above.

3. Select Employees in the list of tables and click the Open button. Access opens the sample Employees table in a table window like the one shown here:

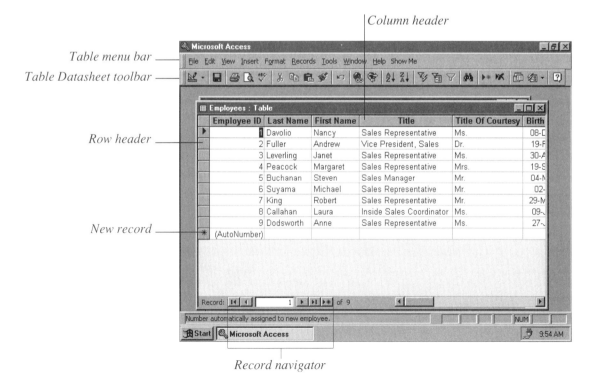

Column header

Table menu bar

Table Datasheet toolbar

Row header

New record

Record navigator

As you can see, Access displays a different toolbar and opens the table in a new window. The table consists of items of information arranged under column headings, called *field names*, that describe the type of information in each column. Each item of information is a *field value*, and each row of items is a *record*. For example, in this table, each item in the Last Name Column is a field value, and each record consists of all the field values for a specific employee.

Fields and records

4. Scroll sideways using the scroll bar in the bottom right corner of the table window. Notice that fields can contain numbers, text, dates, and even graphics (in the Photo field).

Let's close the Northwind database and start one of our own:

1. Click the table window's Close button to close the window.

Closing tables

2. Now click the database window's Close button.

Setting Up a Database

As we work through this book, we'll create a database for a video store owned by Mr. and Mrs. Brock Buster. Before we can enter any information, we need to set up the database so that Access can store all the tables, queries, forms, and reports we'll create in one file. Access comes with many sample databases (see the adjacent tip), but for the Brock Buster's Video database, we'll start from scratch. Follow these steps:

1. Click the New Database button to display this dialog box:

The New Database button

Ready-made databases

Access includes many sample databases that can give you ideas on how to construct your own databases or can be customized to suit your purposes. To use a sample database, click Database Wizard in the opening Microsoft Access dialog box and click OK. Then, on the Databases tab of the New dialog box, double-click any database, and Access will walk you through its construction.

2. With Blank Database selected on the General tab, click OK and then navigate to the My Documents folder. The dialog box looks like this:

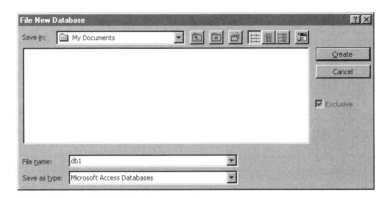

3. Type *Brock Buster's Video* in the File Name edit box and click Create. Access displays this database window:

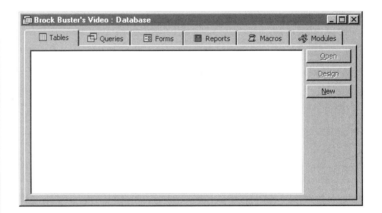

Saving in a different folder

A database file will be saved in the folder designated in the Save In box. If you want to store the file in a different folder, click the arrow to the right of the Save In box, use the drop-down list to navigate to the folder in which you want the file to be saved, and double-click that folder to display its name in the Save In box before you click Save. If the folder you want doesn't exist, you can create one by clicking the Create New Folder button before you save the file. To make this folder the default in Access, choose Options from the Tools menu and type the new folder's path in the Default Database Folder edit box on the General tab. Access will then automatically store all new databases in this folder.

Creating a Table

We can now create our first table, which will be used to maintain customer information. Instead of creating this table from scratch, let's get one of the Access *wizards* to help us. The wizards are tools that walk us through the process of creating standard Access components, such as tables, forms, queries, and reports. (You don't have to use the wizards, but when you are first learning Access, they are a great way to quickly produce components.) Follow these steps:

1. In the database window, click New. Access opens this dialog box, in which you specify how you want to create the table:

2. Click Table Wizard and then click OK to display the first of
   a series of dialog boxes that lead you through the steps of
   creating your table's field structure:

The Table Wizard

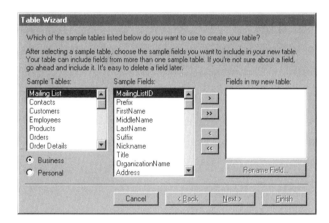

3. In the Sample Tables list, click Customers. The Sample Fields
   list changes to reflect the kind of information usually stored
   in a customer table, with CustomerID selected.

4. Click the > button to add the CustomerID field name to the
   Fields In My New Table list.

5. Select ContactFirstName and click the > button.

6. With ContactFirstName selected in the Fields In My New
   Table list, click Rename Field to display this dialog box:

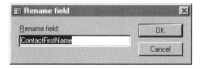

7. Type *First Name* and click OK.

8. Add ContactLastName to the Fields In My New Table list and
   rename it as *Last Name*.

Ready-made business and personal tables

In the first Table Wizard dialog
box, you can choose from a variety of sample tables used in business and at home. The business
tables are listed by default. If you
click the Personal option, Access
displays a list of sample tables you
can create for personal use.

9. Add the BillingAddress, City, StateOrProvince, PostalCode, and PhoneNumber fields. Then rename BillingAddress as *Address* and StateOrProvince as *State*, and click Next to display the following wizard dialog box:

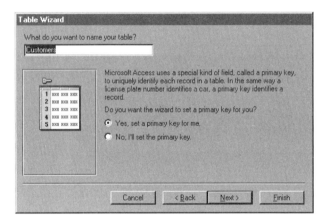

If you make a wrong selection while using a wizard, you can click the Back button to retrace your steps, correct your mistake, and click Next to move forward again.

Primary keys

10. The name Access suggests for this database—Customers—is pretty logical, so don't change the entry in the edit box. Let Access set the *primary key*, which is a field that distinguishes one record from another. When you enter field values in the table, no two entries in the primary key field can be the same. In keyed tables, if you try to enter the same field value in two records, Access displays an error message and won't let you move to a new record until you change one of the duplicates. We will discuss primary keys in more detail in Chapter 4. For now, click Next to display this wizard dialog box:

Allowing Access to create the primary key

If you allow Access to create the primary key, Access inserts an AutoNumber field as the first field of the table. Access then designates that field as the primary key, assigns a field name, and enters a consecutive number as that field's value for each new record.

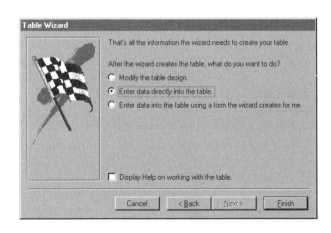

11. You want to enter data directly in the table, so click the Finish button without changing the selected option. Access goes to work setting up the table with the field names you have specified and then displays this table window:

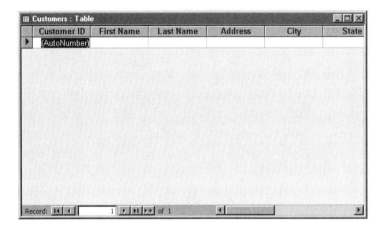

Entering Records in a Table

Each record in the Customers table will contain information about one customer. In Access, we can enter and edit records either directly in the table or in a form. We'll look at tables in this section and cover forms in Chapters 2 and 5.

To enter records in a table, we must first display the table in *datasheet view*. Because we told the Table Wizard that we wanted to enter data directly in the table, Access automatically switched the new table to datasheet view. The arrowhead in the *record selector* (the gray box at the left end of the first row) indicates that the first record is ready to receive data. In the first field of this record, Access has inserted (Auto-Number) to indicate that the program will automatically insert a sequential number in this primary-key field to distinguish this record from all others in the table (see the tip on the facing page). Follow these steps to enter three records in the database:

◄——— Datasheet view

◄——— Record selector

1. Press Enter to confirm (AutoNumber) as the first field's value and move to the next field. Then type *Jock* as the First Name field value. The arrowhead in the row selector changes to a pencil, indicating that the data in the record has been changed but not yet saved. (Access has added a second record with an

asterisk in its row selector, indicating that the new record is empty.) Press Enter to move to the next field.

2. Enter these field values in the first record, pressing Enter after each value:

First Name	Last Name	Address	City	State	Postal Code	Phone Number
	Nicholson	123 Joker Street	Hollywood	CA	11403	2135551111

In the Postal Code field, Access appends a hyphen to the value, and in the Phone Number field, the program puts parentheses around the area code and a hyphen after the 5s (the tip below tells you why). When you press Enter after typing the phone number, Access moves the insertion point to the first field of the next record.

3. Enter two more records, again pressing Enter after each value:

First Name	Last Name	Address	City	State	Postal Code	Phone Number
Laura	Baccall	1171 Whistle Heights	Hollywood	CA	11403	2135559297
Mel	Gibsand	5941 Warrior Road	Hollywood	CA	11403	2135550909

The table's structure

When you use the Table Wizard to create a new table, it sets up the table's structure by assigning names to the fields, determining their data type, allocating sizes, and setting various other properties that control the data you enter in the table. This behind-the-scenes structure is most visible in the Phone Number field, where the wizard has specified that you can enter a maximum of ten digits, which will appear in the table with the first three digits enclosed in parentheses and the sixth and seventh digits separated by a hyphen. We tell you more about the underlying structure of tables and how to manipulate it on page 30.

Shouldn't we save our work now? We don't have to because Access has already taken care of that chore for us. Unlike many applications that wait for us to tell them when to save information, Access saves the values in a new or edited record as soon as we move to another record.

Moving Around the Table

We can move around the table using either the mouse or the keyboard. Like most Windows programs, Access automatically adds scroll bars along the bottom and right sides of the window if the table is too wide or too tall to be displayed in its entirety. We can click the scroll arrows to scroll to the left or right one field at a time or up or down one record at a time. Click on either side of the scroll box to scroll one windowful of records at a time.

As well as using the scroll bars, we can click the buttons on either side of the *record indicator* at the bottom of the window to move among records. The Previous Record and

Next Record buttons move us through the table one record at a time, and the First Record and Last Record buttons move us to the first or last record in the table. The New Record button moves us to the first field of the empty record after the last record.

We can move the insertion point to a specific field by clicking the desired location. To select an entire field, click its left border (the pointer will be shaped like a fat cross). Once we have selected a field, we can move to adjacent fields by pressing the Arrow keys. In fact, using the keyboard is often the fastest way to move around a table. Here's a list of the keys we can use:

Moving with the mouse

Moving with the keyboard

Key	Moves
Tab	Horizontally one field at a time
Right and Left Arrows	When a field is highlighted, horizontally one field at a time; otherwise, moves the insertion point one character at a time
Up and Down Arrows	Vertically one field at a time
Home	To the first field in the current record
End	To the last field in the current record
Ctrl+Home	To the first field in the first record
Ctrl+End	To the last field in the last record
Page Down	Down one windowful of records
Page Up	Up one windowful of records
Ctrl+Page Down	To the right one windowful of fields
Ctrl+Page Up	To the left one windowful of fields

Practice moving around the Customers table using the mouse and keyboard. Knowing various navigational methods is useful because we can then select the method most appropriate for a particular situation. As you can imagine, the ability to jump to the beginning or end of a table and to move through records a windowful at a time is especially useful with tables that contain thousands of records.

Changing the Table's Data

If our data were a simple list that didn't change, we could keep it on paper. But data is often dynamic, and we need to be able to delete, insert, and otherwise change records to keep a database current. In the next few pages, we show you how

Jumping to a specific record

If you know the number of the record you want to work with, you can select the record number currently displayed in the record indicator box, type the new number, and press Enter to jump straight to that record.

to edit the values in individual fields and insert and delete entire records.

Editing Fields

If we make a mistake while entering a field value, we can simply use the Backspace key to delete the error and then retype the value. If we discover a mistake later, we can click an insertion point in the offending field and use normal editing techniques to make the correction. We can also use one or two editing tricks as we enter values, as you'll see if you follow these steps:

The New Record button

1. Click the New Record button on the toolbar to move to the empty record at the end of the table, and then press Enter to move to the First Name field.

Duplicating values

2. Press Ctrl+' (single quotation mark). Access duplicates the value from the same field of the preceding record in the active field. Press Enter.

Within a table, you can also duplicate values by copying and pasting them. Try this:

The Copy button

The Paste button

1. Select the Last Name value in the third record by clicking its left border, and click the Copy button on the toolbar.

2. Then select the Last Name field in the fourth record by clicking its left border, and click the Paste button.

3. Use either the Ctrl+' or copy-and-paste technique to copy the rest of the field values from the third record into the fourth record.

Now let's edit the fourth record:

1. Double-click Gibsand in the fourth record, replace the highlighted value by typing *Glibson*, and press Enter to highlight the next field.

2. Type *104 Bravo Drive*, press Enter, type *Beverly Hills*, but don't press Enter. The table now looks like this:

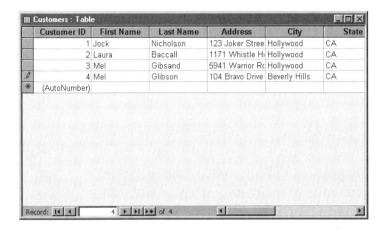

3. Restore the original value in the City field by pressing Ctrl+Z.   ← Undoing edits

4. Here's another way to undo an entry: With Hollywood high-lighted, type *Malibu* in the City field and then press Esc.

5. Press Esc again to restore the original values to all the fields in the record.

Inserting and Deleting Records

To insert a new record in a table, we can click the empty record designated by the asterisk at the end of the table and enter our data. (As you've seen, you can also move quickly to this empty record by clicking the New Record button on the toolbar.) Here's another way to insert a new record:

1. Choose Data Entry from the Records menu. Access displays a single record in which you enter your data, as shown here:

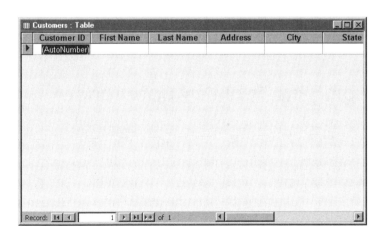

Copying and pasting cautions

Copying and pasting one field value is simple enough, but complications can arise when copying multiple fields. After selecting the fields and clicking the Copy button, you must select the same number of fields before clicking the Paste button. Be careful to paste the field values into fields that have the same properties as the source fields; otherwise data may be lost or Access may refuse to complete the operation. If Access encounters problems, it alerts you and puts the offending values in a Paste Errors table, which you can then evaluate for trouble-shooting clues.

2. Press Enter, and then type the following data, pressing Enter after each field:

First Name	Last Name	Address	City	State	Postal Code	Phone Number
Judy	Foster	5454 Silencio Avenue	Hollywood	CA	11403	2135556819

3. Choose Remove Filter/Sort from the Records menu to see the entire table. (We talk about filters on page 57 and about sorting on page 21.) The new record has been added to the bottom of the table to maintain sequential order in the primary-key Customer ID field.

Deleting records

To delete a record, we simply select the record and click the Delete Record button. Follow these steps to delete the duplicate record for Mel Gibsand from the Customers table:

The Delete Record button

1. Select the fourth record by clicking its record selector, and click the Delete Record button on the toolbar or press the Delete key. Access displays this dialog box:

> **Microsoft Access**
>
> ⚠ You are about to delete 1 record(s).
>
> If you click Yes, you won't be able to undo this Delete operation.
> Are you sure you want to delete these records?
>
> [Yes]   [No]

2. Click Yes. Access deletes the record and updates the table.

Caution!

Be careful when deleting records. If you make a mistake and delete the wrong record, you can't restore the record by clicking an Undo button or choosing Undo from the Edit menu once you've confirmed the deletion.

Deleting records with an AutoNumber field

When you delete a record in a table that has an AutoNumber field, Access does not update the remaining fields' sequential numbers. Once a number has been assigned to a record, that number is never used again, and deleting a record leaves a gap in the sequential order of the values in the AutoNumber field.

Changing the Table's Appearance

Like most people, you're probably more interested in using database tables to store the information you need than in making your data look fancy, but sometimes a little customization can actually make tables easier to work with. This type of customization changes the way the table looks but doesn't alter its data.

Sizing Windows, Columns, and Rows

To see the information in a table, we may have to enlarge the table window or adjust the sizes of fields. Perhaps you've noticed that as you move your mouse around the screen, the pointer sometimes changes shape. On the frame of a window, on the gridlines between the field names, and on the dividing lines between the row selectors, the pointer changes to various kinds of double-headed arrows. While the pointer has this shape, we can resize the table window or the fields.

To resize the window, simply point to its frame, and when the pointer changes to a double-headed arrow, hold down the left mouse button and drag the frame to decrease or increase the window's size.

Sizing windows

Resizing fields is equally simple, as you'll see if you follow these steps:

1. Move the pointer to the gridline between the Address and City field names.

Sizing columns

2. When the pointer changes to a double-headed arrow, hold down the left mouse button and drag to the right. When the line attached to the pointer is about where you want the field's border to be, release the mouse button.

3. Point to the dividing line between the first and second row selectors and drag downward to increase the heights of all the fields in all the records. (You can't adjust the height of only one record.)

Sizing rows

Here's another way to change the widths of fields:

1. Scroll the table until the last four fields are visible. Move the pointer to the City field name, and when the pointer changes to a downward-pointing arrow, click to select that field in all records. Then move the pointer to the Phone Number field name, hold down the Shift key, and click to add the State, Postal Code, and Phone Number fields to the selection.

2. Choose Column Width from the Format menu to display the dialog box shown on the next page.

Fast column width adjustment

Clicking an insertion point in a field, choosing the Column Width command from the Format menu, and clicking the Best Fit option adjusts the width of the column to fit its widest field value. You can also double-click the gridline to the right of the field name's column header.

3. Type *15* and press Enter to change the widths of all four fields at the same time.

The Format menu also includes a Row Height command that allows us to set the heights of the rows precisely. Here's how to restore the original heights of the rows:

Restoring row height →

1. Choose Row Height from the Format menu to display this dialog box:

2. Click the Standard Height check box and then click OK.

You might want to take a moment or two to practice resizing the fields of the Customers table; for example, try shrinking the fields enough to see all of them at one time.

Moving Fields

By default, the fields are displayed in the order in which we entered them when we created the table. We can change the field order by selecting a field's column and dragging it to a new position. For example, if we want to look up a customer's phone number, it might be useful to see the Phone Number field next to the customer names. Follow these steps to move the Phone Number field:

1. Click any field to remove the highlighting, and then click the Phone Number field name to select the entire column.

2. If the Last Name field is out of sight, adjust your view of the table so that you can see both fields.

3. Point to the Phone Number field name, hold down the left mouse button, and drag the field to the left. As you move the

Freezing and hiding fields

You can freeze a single field in position while scrolling other fields. Click anywhere in the field and then choose Freeze Columns from the Format menu. The field moves to the left to become the first column in the table. You can then scroll the remaining fields. Choose Unfreeze All Columns to remove the freeze, and then, if necessary, drag the column back to its original location. To freeze a set of fields, click the first field in the set, hold down the Shift key, click the last field, and then choose Freeze Columns. You can hide fields by selecting them and choosing Hide Columns from the Format menu. To redisplay the fields, choose Unhide Columns from the Format menu, click the check boxes for the fields you want to redisplay, and then click Close to exit the Unhide Columns dialog box.

field, Access highlights the dividing lines between columns to indicate the new position of the Phone Number field.

4. When the dividing line to the right of the Last Name field is highlighted, release the mouse button. Here is the Phone Number field in its new position (we've scrolled the table):

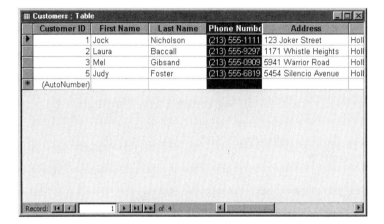

5. For more practice, move the Phone Number field back to its original position to the right of the Postal Code field.

Sorting Records

The Customers table is short enough that we can view all its records in the window at one time. But database tables can contain several hundred or even several thousand records. When working with a large table, we may want to sort the table on a particular field. Here's how to sort the records of the Customers table based on the Last Name field:

1. Click anywhere in the Last Name column and then click the Sort Ascending button on the toolbar to sort starting with A (or the lowest digit), or click the Sort Descending button to sort starting with Z (or the highest digit).

The Sort Ascending and Sort Descending buttons

2. Restore the original order by clicking anywhere in the Customer ID column and clicking the Sort Ascending button.

To sort the records on more than one column, we must first arrange the columns so that they appear side-by-side in the table in the order of the sort. For example, to sort a mailing list in ascending order by state and then by city, we first move

Sorting on more than one column

the State column to the left of the City column. Then we select both columns and click the Sort Ascending button. Access sorts the records first by state and then by city within each state. After the sort, we can move the State column back to the right of the City column.

Other Customizable Options

We can customize several parts of the Access window, as well as control other table functions and properties, by choosing the Options command from the Tools menu. We won't make any changes now, but we will take a look at the dialog box that Access displays when we choose this command:

1. Choose Options from the Tools menu to display the dialog box shown here:

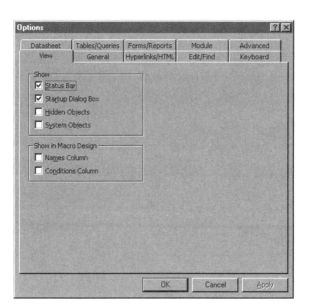

As you can see, the Options dialog box has several tabs, and clicking a tab displays a category of options.

2. For now, take a careful look at what's available for each category so that as you use Access you'll know where to go if you want to change an option. Then click Cancel.

Changing the Font

One way to change the look of a table is to change the font used for the field values. You may have noticed in the Options

Changing cell attributes

As well as changing the font used to display values in datasheet view, you can change the look of the "cells" containing the field values. For example, the gridlines that separate the columns and rows in an Access table are optional. You can remove them by choosing the Cells command from the Format menu and deselecting the horizontal and vertical check boxes in the Gridlines Shown section of the Cells Effects dialog box. Other options control the look of the cells, as well as their color.

dialog box that the Datasheet tab has several font options. We can also change the font, size, and style of the entire table by using menu commands. Follow these steps:

1. Choose Font from the Format menu to display the Font dialog box shown here (your fonts may be different):

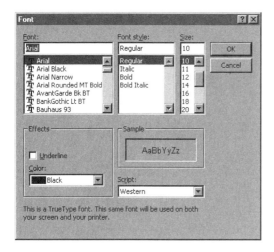

2. In the Font Style section, click Bold, and then click OK to see the result. All the field values in the table are now bold. (You cannot use the Font command to change only part of the table.)

Making field values bold

3. Go ahead and experiment with some of the font options to see how easily you can change the font and font size and draw lines under field values to make them stand out. Return the table to its original settings—Arial, Regular, and 10, with no underline—when you've finished.

Printing Tables

Sometimes we might need a printed copy of a database table for use away from our computer. Before we print, however, we will want to check the layout of the table so that we print in the most efficient way. Otherwise, we may find a table spreading across several pages when a little planning could have kept the table to one or two pages. Follow these steps to check the layout of the Customers table:

1. Click the Print Preview button on the toolbar to display page 1 of the database table, as shown on the next page.

The Print Preview button

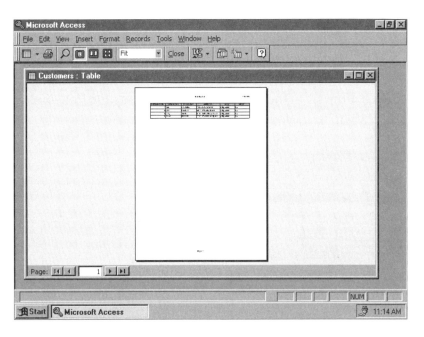

2. Click the Next Page button to the right of the page indicator in the bottom left corner of the window to view the second page, or click the Two Pages button on the Print Preview toolbar to see the first and second pages side by side.

The Two Pages button

To make the entire table fit on one page, we can adjust the page layout in a variety of ways. Try this:

Adjusting page layout

1. Choose Page Setup from the File menu to see this dialog box:

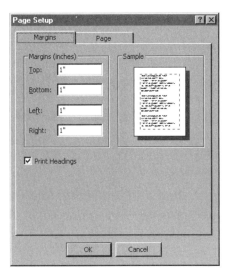

Setting margins

You can adjust the settings on the Margins tab to manipulate the position of the data and how much will print on one page.

2. Click the Page tab to display its options, click Landscape to print the table sideways on the page, and click OK. The print preview window now shows that the table fits on one page.

Changing page orientation

To print one copy of the entire table, all we have to do is click the Print button on the toolbar. If we want to print more than one copy or only part of a table, here's what we do:

The Print button

1. Choose Print from the File menu to display this dialog box, which looks similar to those used by most Windows 95 applications:

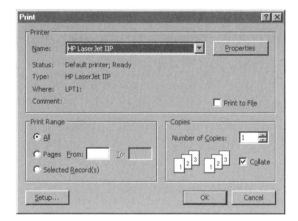

2. Make your selections and click OK. (If you decide not to print, click Cancel or the Close button.) Your printed results should look like those shown at the beginning of the chapter.

3. Click the Close button to leave print preview.

Getting Help

This has been a whistle-stop tour of Access tables, and you might not remember everything we've covered. If we forget how to carry out a particular task, help is never far away. We can use the ToolTips feature to jog our memory about the functions of toolbar buttons. And you may have noticed that dialog boxes contain a Help button you can click to get information about their options. Here we'll look at ways to get information using the Office Assistant, a new feature of the Office 97 applications. Follow the steps on the next page.

Using the Web for help

If you have a modem and are connected to the Internet, you can quickly access Microsoft's Web site to get help or technical support. Simply choose Microsoft On The Web from the Help menu to display a submenu, and then choose the appropriate option.

1. Click the Office Assistant button on the toolbar. The Office Assistant appears, giving you several options on how to proceed:

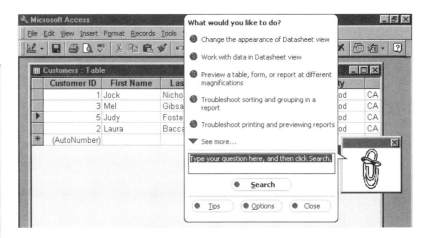

More about the Office Assistant

If the Office Assistant button displays a light bulb, the Office Assistant has a tip for you. Click the button and then click the light bulb in the Office Assistant box to see the tip. If you want to leave the Office Assistant open, you can move it by dragging its title bar, and you can size it by dragging its frame (only two sizes are available). You can then display the search box by clicking its title bar. If having the Office Assistant on the screen bothers you, or if you want to customize it, click the Office Assistant's Options button to open the Office Assistant dialog box. Here, you can select and deselect various options that control when the Office Assistant appears, whether it makes sounds, and what tips it displays. If you want the Office Assistant to appear only when you click the Office Assistant button on the Standard toolbar, deselect the Respond To F1 Key, Help With Wizards, and Display Alerts options in the Assistant Capabilities section on the Options tab. On the Gallery tab, click the Next button to scroll through different animated choices for the assistant (the default is the paper clip) and then click OK to make your change. (You will need to insert your installation disk to complete the switch.)

The Office Assistant displays options that deal with the most recent tasks you have completed. (If you don't find any of the options helpful, you can type a question in the Search box and then click the Search button to have the Office Assistant look up topics that most closely match your question.)

2. Click See More and then click the Preview Two Or More Pages At A Time option to display this Help window:

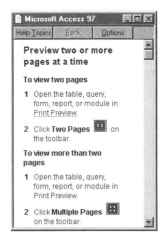

3. Read through the information on how to complete the task, click the Close button, and then click the Office Assistant's Close button.

If we prefer to access Help without the aid of the Office Assistant, we can use the Help menu. Follow these steps:

1. Choose Contents And Index from the Help menu and, if necessary, click the Index tab to display this dialog box:

Searching the help index

2. In the edit box, type *print*. The list below the edit box scrolls to display topics beginning with the letters you type.

3. In the list of topics under Print Preview, select Viewing Multiple Pages and click the Display button. Help displays the information shown on page 26. Click the Close button.

Ending an Access Session

Well, that's a lot of work for one chapter, and you're probably ready for a break. When we finish working with Access, all we have to do is quit. We don't need to worry about saving the information in open database tables; Access updates the table files one record at a time as we enter or edit records. If we make any changes to the appearance of a table in datasheet view or to its structure in design view, Access asks whether we want to save those changes before it closes the table. Let's quit Access now:

1. Click the Close button at the right end of the Access title bar (not the one for the Customers table window).

2. When Access asks whether you want to save your changes, click Yes.

Other ways to quit

Here are some other ways to quit Access:

● Choose Exit from the File menu.

● Press Alt, press F (the underlined letter in *File* on the menu bar), and then press X (the underlined letter in *Exit* on the File menu).

● Double-click the Control menu icon—the key—at the left end of the Access title bar.

2
Tables and Forms

Display field names or
more readable captions

Specify default entries
to speed up data input

Specify input masks to
control what data can be
entered and how it looks

Customers   6/3/97

Customer #	First Name	Last Name	Address	City	State	Zip	Phone #
001	Jock	Nicholson	123 Joker Street	Hollywood	CA	11403	(213) 555-1111
002	Laura	Baccall	1171 Whistle Heights	Hollywood	CA	11403	(213) 555-9297
003	Mel	Gibsand	5941 Warrior Road	Hollywood	CA	11403	(213) 555-0909
005	Judy	Foster	5454 Silencio Avenue	Hollywood	CA	11403	(213) 555-6819
006	Kevin	Custer	2001 Waterworld Drive	Hollywood	CA	11403	( ) 555-2376
007	Sarah	Stone	The Sliver Estates	Hollywood	CA	11403	(213) 555-3737

New Movies   Enter the information for one movie. (The computer will automatically assign an ID number.)

ID   1   Movie Name The Searchers

Date Released 1956 Genre   Western

Retail Price $45.00 Rating   G
                                PG
                                R
                                NONE

Change how
information looks
on-screen but not
the underlying data

Create customized forms to
guide data entry in tables

I n Chapter 1, we learned how to create a database table using the Table Wizard and how to enter and edit records. We saw that tables created this way come with a predetermined structure that controls the kind of data we can enter and the way it looks in the table. In this chapter, we go behind the scenes to examine table structure more closely. We show how to change the structure and how to give the tables we create from scratch the appropriate structure.

Also in this chapter, we round out our discussion of ways to enter data by taking a look at forms, which can greatly facilitate data input.

Editing Table Structure

When we used the Table Wizard to set up the Customers table, the wizard made a number of decisions about the table's design. But those decisions aren't cast in stone. Let's examine the structure of the Customers table and see how to change it:

1. Start Access and open the database you created in Chapter 1 by double-clicking Brock Buster's Video in the list of existing databases at the bottom of the Microsoft Access dialog box.

2. With Customers selected on the Tables tab of the database window, click the Open button. Access opens the Customers table in its own window.

The View button

3. Click the View button on the toolbar to switch to design view. (See the tip below.) Access displays your table's structure in this window:

Switching views

The View button is a toggle that switches between datasheet and design views. Its icon changes depending on which view is active. If you find this toggling business confusing, you can click the arrow to the right of the button and select the view you want from a list.

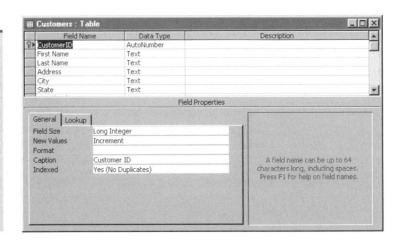

As you can see, the design window is divided into two sections. The top half lists the table's field names, data types, and descriptions (if any). The bottom half lists the properties assigned to the field selected in the top half.

About Data Types

The data type of a field determines what kind of information we can put in the field and how Access can work with the information. You may not want to spend much time learning about all the Access data types now, but we'll introduce the concept here, give you a list of the available types, and leave it to you to explore the different types using online help, as you need them. Follow these steps to take a look at the types used in this table:

1. Press Enter to move to the Data Type column for the CustomerID field.

2. Click the column's arrow button to drop down a list of types   ◄──── Selecting a data type
   like this one:

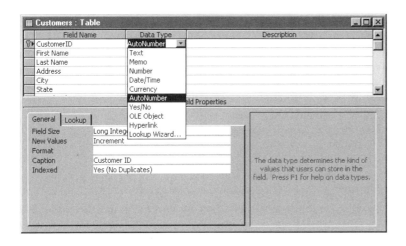

3. With AutoNumber highlighted in the list, press Enter to move
   to the Description column.

4. Type *Sequential number assigned by Access* as this field's   ◄──── Adding field descriptions
   description and then press Enter to move to the next field.
   (This description will appear in the table window's status bar
   when the CustomerID field is active in datasheet view.)

For reference, here's a description of each data type:

Data type definitions ──────────▶

Data Type	Description
Text	General purpose data. Can contain letters, numbers, and other characters such as &, %, =, and ?. Can have up to 255 characters.
Memo	Similar to text, except that size limit is 64,000 characters.
Number	Numeric values that can be assigned these field sizes: *Byte*: Whole numbers between 0 and 255. *Integer*: Whole numbers between –32,768 and 32,767. *Long Integer*: Whole numbers between –2,147,483,648 and 2,147,483,647. *Single*: Single-precision floating-point numbers between –3.402823E38 and –1.401298E–45, and between 1.401298E–45 and 3.402823E38. *Double*: Double-precision floating-point numbers between –1.79769313486231E308 and –4.94065645841247E–324, and between 1.79769313486231E308 and 4.94065645841247E–324. *Replication ID*: Globally unique identifier (GUID)
Date/Time	Valid dates are from January 1, 100 to December 31, 9999, including leap years. Can show dates, times, or both. Can have a variety of formats.
Currency	Numeric values formatted with up to 4 digits to the right of the decimal point and up to 15 to the left. Currency data typically shows negative values in parentheses and has money formatting. Can also be used for fixed-point calculations on numeric values.
AutoNumber	A unique sequential or random numeric value automatically assigned by Access to each new record in the table. Can be assigned a field size of Long Integer or Replication ID. Can be used as the primary key field for tables in which none of the fields have a unique set of values. Cannot be updated.
Yes/No	Use for data that has only two possible values, such as yes/no or on/off.
OLE Object	Can hold a graphic or other object (spreadsheet, sound, video) created with Windows OLE-supporting applications. The object can either be linked to the field or embedded in the field.

Restructure warning

When restructuring a table, bear in mind that some data types cannot be converted to other types without loss of data. Adding a new primary key may result in key violations, and reducing field sizes may result in data loss. If you attempt a restructure that will result in corrupted or lost data, Access advises you of the problem and gives you the choice of continuing or canceling the restructure.

Data Type	Description
Hyperlink	Can be a path to a file on your hard drive, a UNC path to a file on your network server, or a URL to an object on the Internet on an intranet. Access moves to the appropriate destination when you click a hyperlink.
Lookup Wizard	Not a data type. Used to create a field that allows you to look up a value in a different table or select one from a list. See page 40 for an example.

Using Field Properties

Field properties refine field definitions in various ways, and the available properties change depending on the field's data type. We will use some properties frequently, others rarely. In this section, we'll explore the more common properties.

Setting the Field Size

We can set a field size for the text and number data types. For text fields, the size indicates the maximum number of characters we can enter in the field. Up to 255 characters are allowed. If we try to enter, paste, or import a field value that is longer than the specified size, Access truncates the data.

Text field size

Let's set the size of the text fields of the Customers table:

1. In the field grid, click anywhere in the State field to display its properties in the Field Properties section.

2. Double-click 20 in the Field Size edit box to select it, and type 2. Now you can enter no more than two characters, such as the two-letter codes used for US states.

3. Repeat steps 1 and 2 to assign the following field sizes:

Field	Size	Field	Size
First Name	10	City	12
Last Name	12	PostalCode	10
Address	25	PhoneNumber	14

The Field Size property for number fields is different from that of text fields. The size of a number field is determined by the complexity of the format selected (see the table on the facing page). The Customers table doesn't have any number fields, but you'll see how to set the size of number fields later, when you create a different table.

Number field size

Setting the Format

We use the Format property to specify how the characters entered in a field will appear on the screen. Depending on the data type, we may be able to select one of several predefined formats. For some data types we can specify custom formats as well. Follow these steps to tell Access to always display three digits in the CustomerID field:

1. Click anywhere in the CustomerID field and then click the Format edit box in the Field Properties section.

Predefined formats →

2. Click the arrow button to view a list of predefined formats for the AutoNumber data type, and then press Esc to close the list without selecting a format.

Custom formats →

3. Type *000* to tell Access to enter three digits, using zeros unless you enter something else. Now if you enter a CustomerID of *3*, Access will display the entry as *003*.

Specifying an Input Mask

Formats aren't the only way to control the display of data. We can also specify an *input mask*, or character pattern, that determines how our data looks on the screen and what kind of data can be entered in the field. Because we used the Table Wizard to set up the Customers table, Access has already specified input masks for two fields. Let's take a look at these input masks and make any necessary changes:

The Zip code input mask →

1. Click anywhere in the PostalCode field in the field grid to display these field properties:

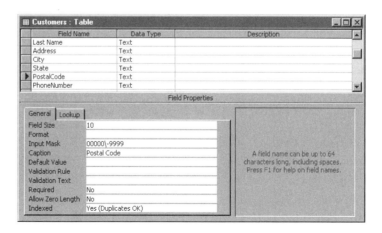

In the Input Mask edit box, the 0s are placeholders for digits you must enter and the 9s are placeholders for optional digits—in this case, a Zip-code extension. The backslash followed by a hyphen indicates that Access will enter the hyphen, whether or not you enter the extension.

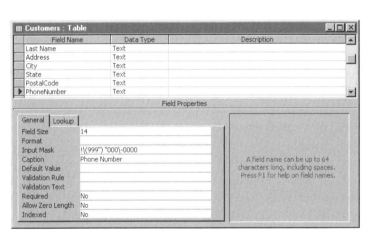

Required and optional digits

2. You are not using Zip-code extensions in the Customers table, so click an insertion point after the last 9, and press Backspace six times to delete all but the five zeros. Now Access will accept only five digits in this field, even though the field size is set to 10.

3. Go ahead and set the Field Size property to 5 to match the input mask.

4. Now click anywhere in the PhoneNumber field to see this more complicated input mask:

The phone number input mask

Again the 0s are required digits, and the 9s are optional digits or spaces. Backslashes precede characters that Access will insert. (The program will also insert the characters enclosed in quotation marks.) The exclamation point tells Access to right-align the characters you enter.

5. Leave this input mask as it is. Because you have already entered optional area codes for all the phone numbers in the table, you don't want to introduce inconsistency by deleting this part of the mask.

On the next page is a list of some characters used in the Input Mask edit box, together with what they mean to Access.

The Input Mask Wizard

If you checked the Advanced Wizards check box when you installed Access, you can use the Input Mask Wizard by clicking the Build button at the right end of the Input Mask edit box (the one labeled with …). Then Access walks you through the different steps in creating a mask. You can preview predefined lists of masks or click Edit List to create your own mask templates, using the characters described on page 36.

Input mask characters

Character	Access's Action
#	Allows any digit, plus and minus signs, and spaces
L	Requires a letter
?	Allows any or no letter
A	Requires a letter or digit
a	Allows any or no letter or digit
&	Requires a character or space
C	Allows any or no character or space
<	Converts all following letters to lowercase
>	Converts all following letters to uppercase
\	Inserts the following character as entered
!	Right-aligns the entry

Let's use some of these characters to enter a couple of new input masks:

1. Click the First Name field in the table grid, and in the Input Mask edit box, type >L<????????? (with nine question marks) to tell Access to allow up to ten letters and to ensure that the first letter is capitalized.

2. Click the Last Name field and enter >L<??????????? (with eleven question marks) as the input mask.

Assigning a Caption

By using the Caption property, we can substitute text for the field name when we display the table. The caption may simply repeat the field name with spaces added for readability, or it may display something different. Let's change a few of the captions specified by the Table Wizard when we created the table:

1. Click anywhere in the CustomerID field to display its properties in the Field Properties section.

2. Click an insertion point to the right of the *D* in *Customer ID* in the Caption edit box, press the Backspace key twice to delete *ID*, and type #.

3. Repeat steps 1 and 2 to change the following captions:

    Postal Code to *Zip*
    Phone Number to *Phone #*

Spaces in field names

In Access, field names can have spaces (see page 11, where we renamed a field as First Name). However, many database programs do not allow spaces in field names. If you might need to export a database to a different program, you may want to assign names with no spaces to the fields and then add spaces in the captions so that the names will be more readable in tables, forms, queries, and reports.

When we display the table, the new captions will be displayed as field names above their respective columns.

Setting a Default Value

The Default Value property lets us specify a field value that Access is to enter in the table automatically. Because the sample video store is small and most of the customers live in the same city, we can use this property for the City, State, and PostalCode fields to speed up data entry. Follow these steps:

1. Click anywhere in the City field to display its properties in the Field Properties section.

2. Click an insertion point in the Default Value edit box and then type *Hollywood* as the default city name.

3. Repeat steps 1 and 2 for the State field and the PostalCode field, specifying *CA* and *11403* as the default values.

Now every record we enter in the new database table will have Hollywood as its City field value, CA as its State field value, and 11403 as its PostalCode field value, unless we replace them with something else.

Requiring Entries

If we leave the table's field structure as it is, it would be possible to create incomplete customer records. To ensure that key information is always entered, we can specify that a field must have an entry. Try this:

1. Click the First Name field, click the Required edit box, click the arrow button, and then select Yes as this property's setting.

2. Repeat step 1 for all the other fields.

Other Properties

Text, number, currency, and date/time fields can all be indexed. When a field is indexed, Access maintains behind-the-scenes lists of entries that allow it to process queries, searches, and sorts based on that field more quickly. (If a few values are repeated often, as is the case in the City, State, and PostalCode fields, then indexing the field doesn't save much

More about the Indexed property

To prevent duplicate values from being entered in a field that is not the table's primary key field, you can set the Indexed property for that field to Yes (No Duplicates). Access automatically specifies this setting for the Indexed property of the primary key field. To view or edit a table's indexes, you can switch to design view and click the Indexes button on the toolbar or choose Indexes from the View menu. In the Indexes window, Access lists the indexed fields. Here, you can edit existing indexes, add new ones, or delete them. (Deleting a field from the Indexes window does not delete the field or its data from the table.) The Indexes window is best used for creating multiple-field indexes. For more information, check Access's online help.

processing time.) Data entry and editing may be slower with indexed fields because Access must maintain the index as well as the table.

We use the three remaining properties in the Field Properties section to check the validity of the data we enter in our tables. The Validation Rule and Validation Text properties are discussed in more detail on page 106. We will rarely need to use the Allow Zero Length property (available for text fields), and we don't set it for any of the fields in this table.

Switching Back to the Table

Now let's return to the table to see the effects of our changes:

1. Click the View button on the toolbar. When Access asks whether you want to save the table, click Yes.

2. Two more dialog boxes appear, one about lost data and the other about data integrity rules. Click Yes in both boxes.

3. Adjust the table window's size and decrease the width of the fields so that you can see all the customer data at once.

The table reflects all the visual changes we made to its structure. The Customer # field displays three digits, and Hollywood, CA, and 11403 have been entered by default in the empty record at the bottom of the table. Let's add one more customer to try everything out:

1. Move to the empty record at the bottom of the table and enter the data below in the indicated fields. (Try typing *kevin* or *KEVIN* instead of *Kevin* or skipping fields to see how Access responds.) Press Enter to skip the City, State, and Zip fields. To skip the phone number's area code, click the field and then use the arrow keys to position the insertion point after the closed parenthesis. Press Enter again to complete the record.

First Name	Last Name	Address	City	State	Postal Code	Phone Number
Kevin	Custer	2001 Waterworld Drive				—-5552376

Here are the results:

Customer #	First Name	Last Name	Address	City	State	Zip	Phone #
001	Jock	Nicholson	123 Joker Street	Hollywood	CA	11403	(213) 555-1111
002	Laura	Baccall	1171 Whistle Heights	Hollywood	CA	11403	(213) 555-9297
003	Mel	Gibsand	5941 Warrior Road	Hollywood	CA	11403	(213) 555-0909
005	Judy	Foster	5454 Silencio Avenue	Hollywood	CA	11403	(213) 555-6819
006	Kevin	Custer	2001 Waterworld Driv	Hollywood	CA	11403	( ) 555-2376
(AutoNumber)				Hollywood	CA	11403	

Creating Tables from Scratch

Although it's often faster to use the Table Wizard to create tables, we need to know how to set up tables on our own for those times when the Access templates don't quite fit the bill. Let's create a table to hold movie information:

1. Close the Customers table, saving your layout changes.

2. With the Tables tab selected in the database window, click New. In the dialog box that pops up, select Design View and then click OK. Access displays an empty window in design view with the insertion point blinking in the first field.

   Starting a new table

3. Type *Movie Name* in the first field and press Enter to move to the Data Type column, where Access suggests Text as the data type. Access has also created some default settings in the Field Properties section.

4. Press Enter twice to accept Text as the data type, skip the Description column, and jump to the next field.

5. Name this field *Date Released*, set its data type to Number, click the Field Size edit box, click the arrow button, and set this property to Integer.

6. Now create these fields:

Field Name	Data Type	Properties
Rating	Text	Field Size = 4
Retail Price	Currency	
Genre	Text	

Since we know that there are only a few ratings to choose from, we can use the Lookup Wizard to create an edit box with a drop-down list that defines all the possible values for this field. Here are the steps for creating this element, which is called a *combo box:*

Combo boxes

The Lookup Wizard

1. Click the Data Type column for the Rating field, click the arrow button, and select Lookup Wizard to display this dialog box:

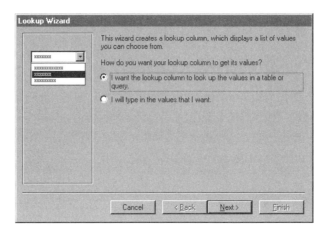

2. Select the option that allows you to type in values and click Next to display this dialog box:

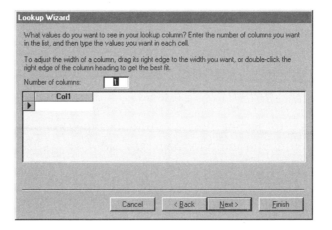

Looking up values in a table

When all the possible values for a field are listed as unique entries in an existing table or query, you can have Access refer to that table whenever you need to select the field value. See page 100 for an example of this type of lookup.

3. Leave Number Of Columns set to 1 and press Tab to move to the empty field in Col1.

4. Enter *G* and press tab. Then enter *PG, R,* and *NONE*, pressing Tab to move to a new field for each rating. Click Next.

5. Leaving the lookup name as Rating, click Finish.

6. In the Field Properties section, click the Lookup tab to display these properties:

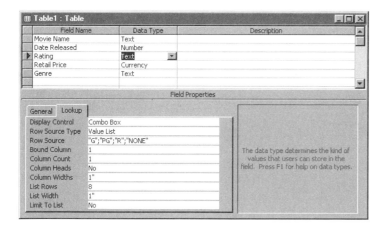

7. Because you want to limit the data in this field to the entries in the lookup list, click the Limit To List edit box and change this property to Yes.

Now let's see how this table looks in datasheet view:

1. Click the View button on the toolbar, click Yes to save the table, and assign *Movies* as its title.

Saving the table

2. When Access asks whether it should create a primary key, click Yes. Access adds an ID field and displays an empty record in datasheet view, ready for you to enter data.

3. Press Enter, type *The Searchers*, press Enter again, type *1956*, and press Enter.

4. In the Rating field, click the arrow button, select NONE from the list, and press Enter.

5. Type *45* as the price, press Enter, type *Western*, and press Enter to end the record. With column widths adjusted, the table looks like this:

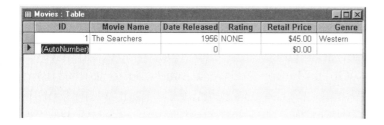

6. Close the table window, saving your layout changes.

Now let's build up our database with another table so that we have something to work with in later chapters:

1. Create a new table in design view with the following fields:

Field Name	Data Type	Properties
Rental Terms	Text	
Days	Number	Field Size = Byte
Cost	Currency	
Daily Fine	Currency	

2. Click the View button on the toolbar, save the table as *Terms*, and click No when Access asks whether it should create a primary key.

3. Then insert the following data in the table:

Rental Terms	Days	Cost	Daily Fine
New Release	1	3.5	10
Oldie Weekend	3	2	5
One Day Oldie	1	1	5

4. Close the table window.

Using Forms to Enter and View Data

By now you are familiar with the procedure for entering data directly in tables, but with many databases it's easier to use forms to input data because they are more intuitive. As a demonstration, we'll create some very simple forms in this chapter. We'll tackle more complex forms in Chapter 5.

Creating AutoForms

For our first form, we'll create an input screen for the Customers table. Follow these steps:

The New Object button

1. With Customers selected on the Tables tab of the database window, click the arrow to the right of the New Object button on the toolbar and then click AutoForm. (You could just click the New Object button but we wanted you to see the list of available objects.) Access generates a form with all of the fields listed in the Customers table and displays the first record from the table, as shown at the top of the facing page.

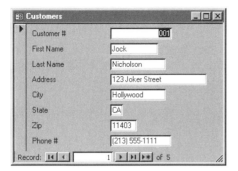

2. Click the New Record button at the bottom of the form window to move to an empty record.

3. With AutoNumber highlighted in the Customer # field, press Enter. Then type the following information, pressing Enter to move from one edit box to another:

First Name	Last Name	Address	City	State	Postal Code	Phone Number
Sarah	Stone	The Sliver Estates				2135553737

4. After you have entered the information, close the form by clicking the window's Close button, and when prompted, save the form as *New Customers*.

Using the Form Wizard

Now let's use a different method to create a form for entering movie information:

1. In the database window, click the Forms tab, which now lists the New Customers form.

2. Click New. Access displays the dialog box shown here:

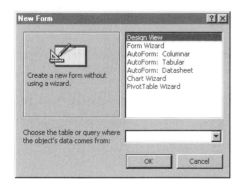

Other autoforms and wizards

In addition to using the Form Wizard, you can create new forms directly in design view. You can also select one of three types of autoforms: Columnar displays fields one above the other from top to bottom, as in the New Customers form you just created; Tabular displays fields from left to right across the form; and Datasheet creates a form with rows and columns like a table. You can also create a form with the Chart Wizard (see page 132) or the Pivot-Table Wizard (see page 149).

The Form Wizard →

3. Select Form Wizard and click OK to display this dialog box, where you select the table on which you want to base the form and the specific fields you want to include:

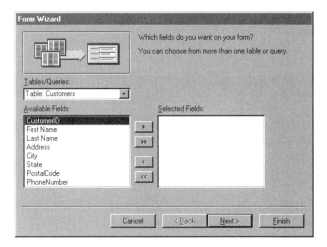

4. Click the arrow to the right of the Tables/Queries edit box and select Table: Movies from the drop-down list. All of the fields in the Movies table are now listed in the Available Fields box.

5. Click the >> button to move all the fields to the Selected Fields box, and then click Next to display the next dialog box:

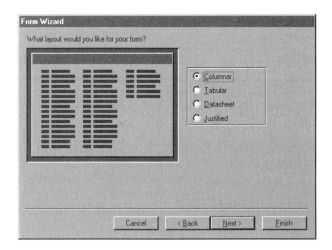

Quick finish

Having selected the table and fields in the first Form Wizard dialog box, you can click the Finish button to accept the default settings in the three remaining dialog boxes and jump directly to the new form's window.

6. Select each layout option to explore what's available, and then select Columnar and click Next. The dialog box shown on the next page appears.

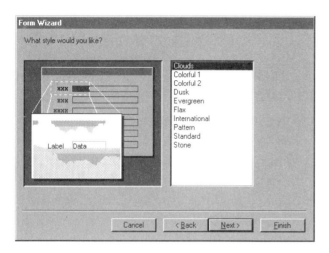

7. Select each style in the list box to see the choices available for the form's background. Then select Standard and click Next to display this dialog box:

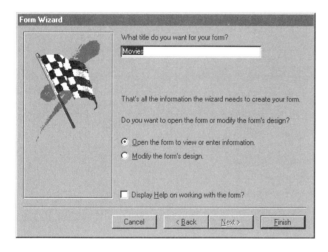

8. Assign *New Movies* as the form's title, and with the Open The Form To View Or Enter Information option selected, click Finish to display your new form, which looks like this:

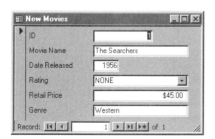

Notice that, because we defined the possible entries for the Rating field using the Lookup Wizard (see page 40), Access automatically displays an arrow button for this field.

Customizing Forms

We have just created a new form, but suppose we want the form to look and act differently than the way Access has set it up. In this section, we demonstrate how to edit the New Movies form to meet your needs. As you follow these steps, save your work often by clicking the Save button, in case of computer crashes or power "hiccups":

The Save button

1. Click the View button on the toolbar to switch to design view. Then, if necessary, click the Maximize button on the form window's title bar to expand the window to fill the screen, like this:

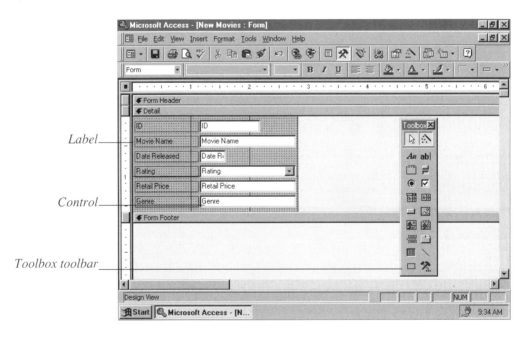

The Toolbox button

2. Close the Toolbox toolbar by clicking the Toolbox button on the Form Design toolbar. (You will use some of these tools later, but you don't need them right now.)

In design view, the form window is divided into three sections: the Form Header, which can contain information such as a title that you want to appear at the top of the form (it's

currently blank); the Detail section, which displays white
boxes called *controls*—where we will enter information in the
new form—and gray boxes called *labels* for each of the fields
we selected for inclusion in the form; and the Form Footer,
which functions like the Form Header. Two other sections,
Page Header and Page Footer, are not visible in the form now
on the screen. They can contain elements we want to appear
on every page of a multi-page form. The window also contains horizontal and vertical rulers and gridlines that help us
position controls and labels on the form.

Controls and labels

Moving Controls and Labels

Let's try rearranging some of the controls and their labels:

1. In the Detail section, move the mouse pointer to the right
   border of the light gray, active area, where the pointer changes
   to a bar with opposing arrows. Hold down the left mouse
   button and drag to the right, releasing the mouse button when
   the active area just fills the form window. (The gray label
   boxes must still be in view.)

Sizing the active area

2. Click the white Movie Name control. Small squares called
   handles appear around the control's border, like this:

Selecting controls

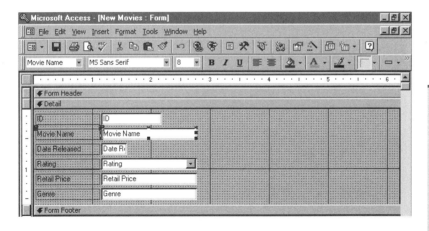

3. With the mouse, point to the border of the selected control,
   and when the pointer changes to a black open hand, hold down
   the left mouse button and drag the control and its label up and
   to the right of the ID control. (You can use the gridlines and
   rulers to help align the controls.)

Two types of hands

To move a control and its label on
a form so that they maintain their
relative positions, select the control, point to the control's border,
and drag the black open hand that
appears. To move a control independently of its label, select the control, point to the large handle in the
control's top left corner, and drag
the black pointing hand that appears. Similarly, to move a label
independently, select the label and
drag the black pointing hand.

4. Now select and drag the Genre control and its label to the right of the Date Released control.

5. Finally, select and drag the Rating control and its label to the right of the Retail Price control. The form now looks like this:

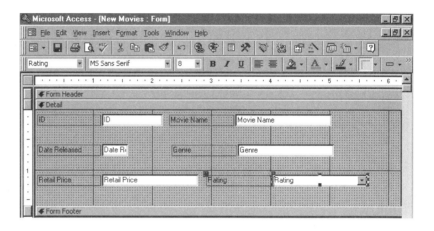

Sizing Controls and Labels

You may have noticed that all the gray label boxes are the same size, and several of the control boxes are too big. Let's fix the sizes now:

1. Select the Date Released label, point to the middle handle on the right side, and when the pointer changes to a double-headed arrow, hold down the left mouse button and drag to the left until the label is just big enough to display its text.

2. Make the boxes for the ID and Retail Price labels the same size as for the Date Released label.

Aligning controls

You can use the Align command on the Format menu to left-align, right-align, top-align, or bottom-align the controls in your forms. First select the control or controls you want to align. Then choose Align from the Format menu and one of the commands from the submenu. You can also align the controls to the nearest gridline by choosing Align and then To Grid.

3. Now adjust the size of the boxes for the ID and Retail Price controls to match the size of the Date Released control. (It's OK that you can't see all of *Date Released* and *Retail Price*.)

4. Select the box for the ID control, point to the large handle in the top left corner, and when the pointer changes to a pointing hand, hold down the left mouse button and drag to the left, moving the control box until it is next to the ID label.

5. Size and rearrange the remaining labels and controls until your form looks like this:

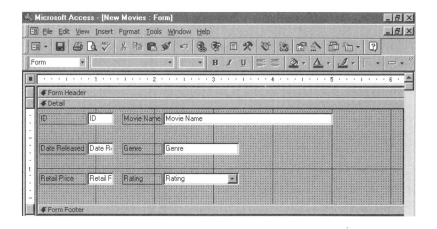

Making Information Stand Out

Now let's change the appearance of the controls:

1. Point to the top of the ruler to the left of the Detail section, and when the pointer changes to a right arrow, hold down the left mouse button and drag downward. When all the labels and controls are contained within the selection area defined by the pointer, release the mouse button. (You can also choose Select All from the Edit menu.) All the labels and control boxes are now selected, as indicated by the handles surrounding them.

Selecting by dragging

2. Click the Bold button on the Formatting toolbar.

The Bold button

3. Suppose you decide the labels shouldn't be bold after all. Click a blank area of the Detail section to remove the selection, click the ID label, hold down the Shift key, and click all the other labels to add them to the selection. Then simply click the Bold button to return the labels to regular style.

Selecting with the Shift key

4. Click a blank area of the Detail section to remove the selection, and then select the Movie Name control.

5. Click the arrow to the right of the Font/Fore Color button on the Formatting toolbar to display a palette of colors, and click the red option in the third row. The text in the Movie Name control box is now red.

The Font/Fore Color button

6. Click the arrow to the right of the Line/Border Color button and select the yellow option from the drop-down palette.

The Line/Border Color button

Changing Formats

The Rating field has only four possible values, so it might be easier to display all of the ratings in a list box rather than a combo box. Let's go ahead and change it:

List boxes

1. Select the Rating control and choose Change To and then List Box from the Format menu.

2. Click the View button to see all the possible choices displayed in the new list box. Then switch back to design view.

3. If you want, resize the list box so that it is just the size needed to display the choices.

Deleting and Adding Controls

When initially designing a form, we may include fields that we don't need (for example, fields with default values). Or we may leave out some fields and later decide to include them. As a demonstration, let's delete a field from the form and then add it again. Follow these steps:

1. Select the Date Released control and press Delete. Access removes the control and its label from the form.

The Field List button

2. Click the Field List button on the Form Design toolbar, click Date Released in the list of fields that appears, and drag the field to the space below the ID control, where it was before.

3. Close the Field List box, resize the label and control to fit, and make the control bold.

Adding a Title

The Form Header section is currently blank, but we can use this section for a title, like this:

Sizing sections

1. In design view, point to the border between the Form Header and Detail sections. When the pointer changes to a double-headed arrow, drag the mouse downward to open up the Form Header section.

2. Choose Toolbox from the View menu to display the Toolbox toolbar, which you closed earlier.

The Label button

3. Click the Label button on the Toolbox toolbar and move the pointer into the Form Header section, where it becomes a cross hair with a large A next to it.

4. Click to position an insertion point, and type *New Movies*.

5. Repeat steps 3 and 4, this time inserting an instructional label to the right of New Movies that contains the following text:

    Enter the information for one movie. (The computer will automatically assign an ID number.)

6. Now right-click the New Movies label and choose Properties from the object menu to display this dialog box:

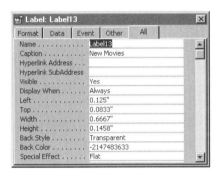

    You might want to take a minute to scroll through the list on the All tab to get an idea of the properties you can set from this dialog box. (The properties are also grouped by category on four other tabs in the dialog box.)

7. Scroll to the Font Name property, click the edit box, click the arrow button, and select Times New Roman. Next change the Font Size property from 8 to 14. Then click the Font Weight edit box, click the arrow button, and select Heavy. Close the Properties dialog box.

Changing the font, font size, and font weight

8. Resize the New Movies label by double-clicking any of its handles.

Sizing labels to fit their text

The Italic button

9. Select the instructional label and click the Italic button on the Formatting toolbar, and then resize the label.

10. Now adjust the positions of the labels by dragging the large handle in the top left corner of each label. (You may have to

turn off the Snap To Grid command on the Format menu to accurately align the text of the labels.) Here are the results:

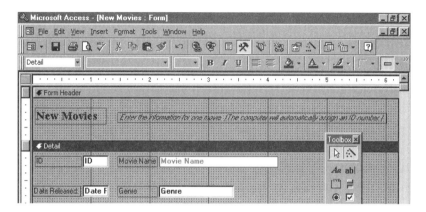

Changing the Input Order

When we move controls around on a form, we need to check that we can still move from field to field in a logical way. Follow these steps to check the form:

1. Click the View button on the toolbar to switch to form view, and then move to a new record.

2. Tab through the controls, and then enter the following data in the correct fields, pressing Enter when you have finished:

Movie Name	Date Released	Genre	Retail Price	Rating
Frankenstein	1993	Horror	45	R

As we have seen, Access still moves through the controls in the order in which the fields appear in the table, even though we have moved them on the form. It also jumps to the ID

More about gridlines and the Grid commands

By default, Access displays gridlines to help you align the controls and labels on your form. You can turn off the gridlines by choosing Grid from the View menu. Whether the gridlines are turned on or off, you can use the Snap To Grid command on the Format menu. You can also choose Align and then To Grid or Size and then To Grid from the Format menu to position or size the controls and labels. If you don't see gridlines when the Grid command is active on the View menu, open the Properties dialog box for the entire form by right-clicking the box at the junction of the horizontal and vertical rulers. Check the Grid X and Grid Y values, which control the number of gridlines per inch. If these values are too large, the grid may be too fine to display. Try changing the values to 10 or 12.

control even though the user cannot change this field. Let's make the order more logical:

1. Click the View button to switch back to design view.

2. Select the ID control and click the Properties button on the Form Design toolbar to see the Properties dialog box.

The Properties button

3. Scroll to the Tab Stop property and change this property to No so that Access will skip the ID control as information is entered. Then close the Properties dialog box.

4. Next, right-click the Date Released control and choose Properties. Scroll to the Tab Index property, which controls the order in which controls are activated when you press Tab, change the setting to 2, and then close the Properties dialog box.

5. Repeat step 4 to change the Tab Index property for Genre to 3, Retail Price to 4, and Rating to 5.

6. Switch back to form view and tab through the controls, which are now activated sequentially.

Now that we have created a usable custom form, let's enter some more movie data:

1. Move to a new record and enter the following films (and any others that you would like):

Movie Name	Date Released	Genre	Retail Price	Rating
Cinderella	1950	Family	45	G
Frankenstein	1931	Horror	65	NONE
Star Wars	1977	Action	25	PG
Casablanca	1942	Drama	35	NONE
Braveheart	1995	Drama	19.99	R

2. Close the database, saving your changes to the New Movies form when prompted.

Now that you have a solid grasp of creating tables and inputting data, we can show you how to manipulate the data to get useful information out of the database. In the next chapter, we'll look at queries and reports, and we'll also show you how to use switchboards to move among database components.

Queries, Reports,
and Switchboards

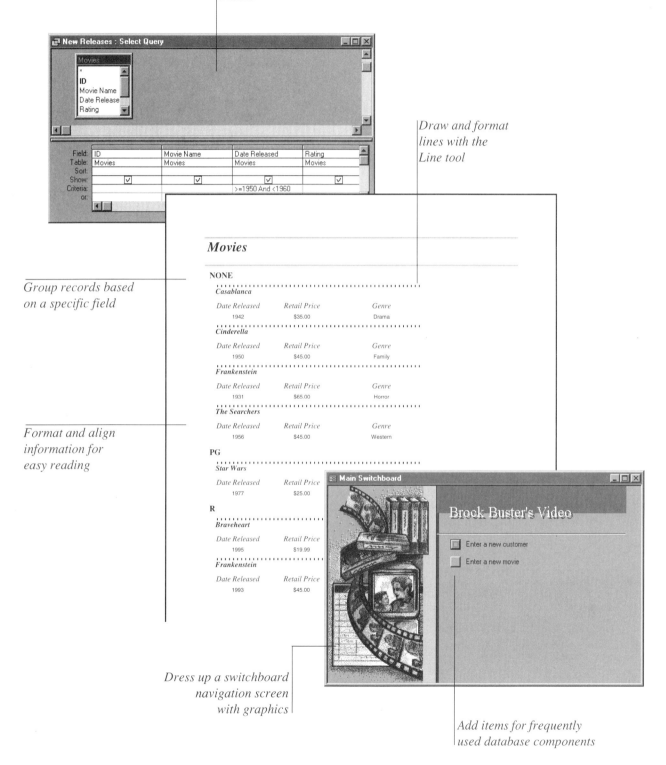

Use a select query to extract records from a table

Draw and format lines with the Line tool

Group records based on a specific field

Format and align information for easy reading

Dress up a switchboard navigation screen with graphics

Add items for frequently used database components

New Releases : Select Query

Movies
ID
Movie Name
Date Release
Rating

Field:	ID	Movie Name	Date Released	Rating
Table:	Movies	Movies	Movies	Movies
Sort:				
Show:	☑	☑	☑	☑
Criteria:			>=1950 And <1960	
or:				

Movies

NONE

Casablanca

Date Released	Retail Price	Genre
1942	$35.00	Drama

Cinderella

Date Released	Retail Price	Genre
1950	$45.00	Family

Frankenstein

Date Released	Retail Price	Genre
1931	$65.00	Horror

The Searchers

Date Released	Retail Price	Genre
1956	$45.00	Western

PG

Star Wars

Date Released	Retail Price
1977	$25.00

R

Braveheart

Date Released	Retail Price
1995	$19.99

Frankenstein

Date Released	Retail Price
1993	$45.00

Main Switchboard

Brock Buster's Video

☐ Enter a new customer

☐ Enter a new movie

At this stage, you have learned how to create a database and to input information using tables and forms. In this chapter, we look at ways of extracting information using the simple Find command and filtering tools, as well as more complex queries and reports. We also examine switchboards, which allow us to move among forms, queries, and reports in a more intuitive way.

Using Find and Filters

Using the Find button is the simplest way to find specific information that we know is in a database. For example, to find the film Casablanca in the Brock Buster's Video database, follow these steps:

1. If necessary, start Access and open the Brock Buster's Video database.

2. From the Tables tab, open the Movies table.

The Find button

3. Click the Find button on the toolbar to display this dialog box:

4. Type *Casablanca* in the Find What edit box, deselect the Search Only Current Field option so that Access will search all fields, and click Find First. Access highlights Casablanca in the table. (To see the result, you may need to move the Find dialog box by dragging its title bar.)

Moving dialog boxes

If we are not sure of the exact title of the movie, we can also use the Find button to find parts of an entry, like this:

Finding part of a field value

1. Replace Casablanca with *heart* in the Find What box, change the Match setting to Any Part Of Field, and click Find Next. Access highlights the *heart* in *Braveheart*.

2. Take a few minutes to familiarize yourself with the options in the Find dialog box and experiment with this useful tool on your own. Then click the Close button to close the dialog box.

When dealing with a very large table, we can temporarily focus on a subset of records that have something in common by using *filters*. Follow these steps to see how filters work:

1. In the Movies table, double-click NONE in the Rating field of the Casablanca record.

2. Click the Filter By Selection button on the toolbar. Access displays only those films with NONE as their rating.

The Filter By Selection button

3. Click the Remove Filter button to redisplay all the records in the table.

The Remove Filter button

4. As another example, highlight only *195* in the Date Released field of the Cinderella record and then click the Filter By Selection button to see only the movies made in the '50s. Then click the Remove Filter button again to redisplay all the records.

Using Queries

Suppose Mrs. Buster wants a list of all of the movies and their retail prices. She doesn't want the ID, Date Released, Rating, or Genre information. To give Mrs. Buster what she wants, we will need to use a query. Queries are more complex than filters, but they are by far the most flexible way to search a database. Access provides two types of queries: select queries can find and extract information from a database, and action queries can update or delete records. In this section, we'll look at some simple select queries. In Chapter 5, we'll show you some more complex queries, and then in Chapter 6, we'll look at some action queries.

Here are some examples of common select queries:

- A supervisor might want a list of the emergency contacts for all the employees in his or her department.

- A sales manager might want to see the records for sales over a certain dollar amount.

- A training instructor might want to identify classes for which too few or too many people have enrolled.

More about filters

Filter By Selection can be used in tables, forms, and queries. You can even use filters within filters by first using one criterion and then filtering the results using a second criterion. For example, in a longer movie list, you might want to find all the Westerns that were made in the '50s. If you can't easily select the criteria in the table for filtering, click the Filter By Form button on the toolbar to set up filters using drop-down lists. When you are not sure whether a certain criterion exists in a longer table, you can use the Filter For command. For example, to check if the Movies table contains any PG-13 rated movies, right-click the Rating field, type *PG-13* in the Filter For box on the object menu, and press Enter. Access displays only the records that meet the specified criterion.

- A purchasing officer might want a list of vendors who carry all the supplies needed for a particular job so that one order can be placed instead of several.

Access answers a select query by identifying the subset of records and fields that meet the query's criteria and placing the subset in a temporary table called a *query datasheet*.

Query datasheets →

Selecting Specific Fields

Let's go ahead and create the query that asks for every movie and its retail price. Follow these steps:

1. Click the arrow to the right of the New Object button on the toolbar and select Query from the drop-down list.

2. Access warns you that you must save the Movies table before creating the query. Click Yes. Access displays this dialog box:

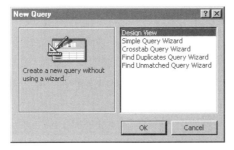

The Simple Query Wizard →

3. Click Simple Query Wizard and then click OK. Access displays this dialog box:

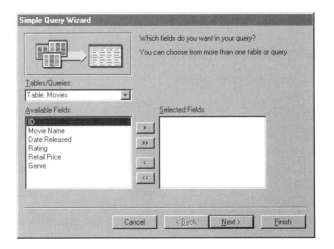

Other query wizards

The other options in the New Query dialog box guide you through the process of creating different types of queries. We deal with crosstab queries in a separate tip on page 148. The Find Duplicates and Find Unmatched Query Wizards help you set up queries to find potential errors in the design of your database. If you are thinking about redesigning a database, you may want to explore these queries after reading Chapter 4.

4. With Table: Movies selected in the Tables/Queries box, click Movie Name in the Available Fields list and then click the > button to move it to the Selected Fields box. Repeat this step for Retail Price and click Next.

5. In the next dialog box, leave the Detail option selected and click Next.

6. Assign *Movie Prices* as the query's title and, with the Open The Query To View Information option checked, click Finish. Access runs the query and displays this query datasheet:

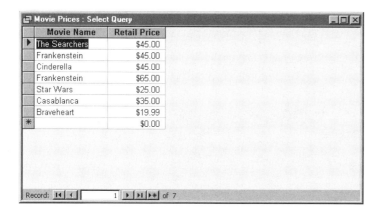

7. If you want, you can print the query datasheet for Mrs. Buster by clicking the Print button on the toolbar.

Printing query results

8. Click the Close button to close the query window.

The Queries tab of the database window now lists Movie Prices as an existing query. Any time we want a list of movies and their prices, we can select this query on the Queries tab and click Open to have Access run the query and display a new datasheet of results. If we have made changes to the Movies table, these changes will be reflected in the new datasheet.

Rerunning saved queries

Selecting Specific Records

We now know how to ask questions that require Access to select fields from a table. What if we want Access to select fields from specific records only? For example, suppose a customer wants a list of all the action films with a PG rating. Follow the steps on the next page to obtain this list.

No entries in query datasheets

The query datasheet has an empty record at the bottom. An inexperienced user might add partial records to the table on which the query is based by making entries in this record. To avoid this kind of partial updating from a query, be sure that all of the table's fields require an entry (see page 37).

Creating new queries →

1. On the Queries tab, click New to display the New Query dialog box, click Design View, and then click OK to display this dialog box, where you specify the table you want to work with:

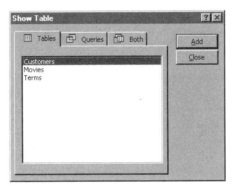

Specifying a table →

2. On the Tables tab, select Movies, click Add, and click Close. You then see this query design window:

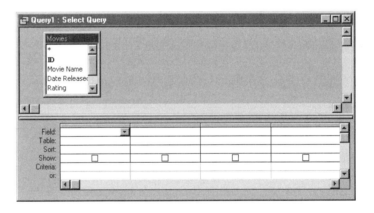

In the top half of the window, a Movies box lists the fields in the Movies table. (The * at the top of the list represents all the fields.) Below is a table grid called the *query by example (QBE) grid*, in which you can visually construct the query.

Query by example grid →

Adding a field →

3. In the Movies box, double-click the Movie Name field to tell Access to include Movie Name field values in the results of your query. Access transfers the Movie Name field to the first column of the QBE grid's Field row, identifies the field's table in the Table row, and displays a checkmark in the box in the Show row to indicate that Movie Name field values will appear in the query datasheet.

4. Double-click Rating in the Movies box to transfer it to the second column of the QBE grid. Then scroll the Movies box and double-click Genre. (If you double-click the wrong field name, press the Delete key to delete the highlighted entry, and then try again.)

5. With the Show boxes of these three fields selected, click the Run button on the toolbar. Here's the result:

The Run button

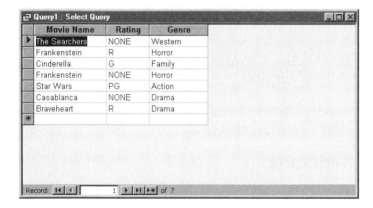

Some of these movies are not PG-rated action films, so we still have some work to do on this query. Follow these steps:

1. Click the View button on the toolbar to return to the query design window.

Modifying queries

2. Click the Criteria row of the Rating column and type *pg*.

3. Then click the Criteria row of the Genre column, type *ACTION*, and click the Or field below to see the new query criteria:

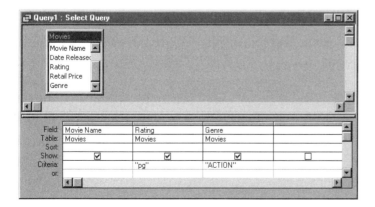

The Table row

When you are working with the fields from just one table, you don't need to display the Table row in the QBE grid. To turn it off, deselect Table Names from the View menu.

You are telling Access to select the records that have both the value PG in the Rating field and the value Action in the Genre field, and to display the values from the Movie Name, Rating, and Genre fields in the datasheet. Notice that the Criteria row is not case sensitive (you can use capital or lowercase letters), and that Access has enclosed the criteria in quotation marks.

Turning off field display →

4. It's not really necessary to include the Rating and Genre values in the result of this query, so click the Show check boxes for these columns to remove their check marks.

5. Click the Run button. As you can see, Star Wars is the only movie that meets the query criteria.

6. Close the query window, saving the query as *PG Action Movies* when Access prompts you.

Using Wildcards

Suppose a customer wants to know if Brock Buster's Video has a particular movie. The customer can remember what the movie is about but not the movie's name, except that it begins with the letter *C*. We can search for all the movies beginning

The * wildcard →

with *C* by using a query with the * wildcard, a placeholder that represents any character or characters. Let's create this query now:

1. From the Queries tab of the database window, create a new query using design view.

2. Add the Movies table to the query design window and then close the Show Table dialog box.

Adding all the fields →

3. Double-click the title bar of the Movie box. All of the fields are highlighted.

4. Point to the selected fields, hold down the left mouse button, drag the pointer over the QBE grid, and release the mouse button. Access enters the fields in the columns of the grid in the order in which they appear in the table.

5. In the Criteria row of the Movie Name column, type *C** and press the Tab key to move to the next column. Access changes

the criteria to *Like "C*"*. The * wildcard tells Access to look for a field value that starts with *C* and is followed by any number of additional characters. Because you are not looking for an exact match, Access clarifies the criteria by preceding it with the Like operator.

6. Run the query. Access displays this datasheet:

ID	Movie Name	Date Released	Rating	Retail Price	Gen
5	Cinderella	1950	G	$45.00	Family
6	Casablanca	1942	NONE	$35.00	Drama
(AutoNumber)		0		$0.00	

Record: |◄| ◄| 1 |►|►I|►*| of 2

As you can see, the * wildcard is useful when we need to find records that are similar but not the same. We can place the * wildcard before, after, and between characters, and we can use it more than once in a single field. For example, we could have used the criterion *Like "C*B*"* in the Movie Name field to find only Casablanca.

In addition to *, we can use the ? wildcard as a placeholder for one character. For example, we could find Frankenstein by typing *Frank???????* in the Criteria row of the Movie Name column of a query.

The ? wildcard

Both the * and the ? wildcards can be used to locate records when we are unsure of the spelling of a field value, and the more information we can supply, the more specific the query datasheet will be. For example, there may be dozens of movies beginning with *C* in a true movie database, but we could easily narrow the search for Casablanca by typing *C** as the Movie Name criterion and *Drama* as the Genre criterion.

Editing Query Datasheets

If you entered the information for the Movies table exactly as it is shown on page 53, the Movies table contains an error.

Cinderella was made in 1950 and the Motion Picture Association of America did not begin rating films until 1966, so Cinderella should have a NONE rating. If we correct the record in the query datasheet that results from running the *Like "C*"* query, Access automatically corrects the record in the table. Try this:

1. Click the Rating field in the Cinderella record to display an arrow button.

2. Click the arrow button, select NONE from the drop-down list, and click a different record.

The Database Window button →

3. Click the Database Window button on the toolbar, open the Movies table, and verify that the Cinderella record has been updated. Then close the table and choose the query from the Window menu to redisplay it.

Using Mathematical Operators

Access allows us to use mathematical operators in criteria, including = (equal to), < (less than), > (greater than), <= (less than or equal to), and >= (greater than or equal to). These operators are often used for such tasks as identifying customers whose orders fall within a certain range. Let's try using a mathematical operator with the Date Released field to find all the movies in stock that were made after 1990:

1. Switch to design view and delete the criterion in the Movie Name column.

2. In the Criteria row of the Date Released column, type *>1990*.

3. Run the query. Access displays a datasheet for the two movies that were made after 1990.

Saving queries →

4. Click the Save button on the toolbar. Because you have not yet given this query a name, Access displays the Save As dialog box.

5. Save this query as *New Releases*.

Using Logical Operators

As you saw on page 61, we can narrow down the focus of a
query by specifying criteria in more than one field of the QBE
grid. Sometimes we might want to extract records that meet
all of the specified criteria in all the fields (this *And* that), and
sometimes we might want to extract records that meet any of
the criteria (this *Or* that). Let's look at a few examples.

The And Operator

Suppose we want only the movies that were made in the '50s.
We can't simply change the criterion from our previous query
to >1950. Instead, we must construct a range by using the And
operator. Follow these steps:

1. Switch to design view and change the criterion in the Date   **Using one field**
   Released field to *>=1950 And <1960*. The QBE grid looks
   like this:

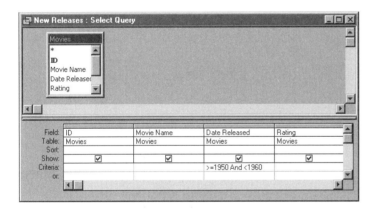

2. Run the query. The New Releases datasheet shows only the
   two movies made in the '50s.

   Now follow these steps to get a list of Westerns made in the
   '50s by using an additional criterion:

1. Switch back to design view, leave the criteria in the Date   **Using more than one field**
   Released column as they are, and type *Western* in the Criteria
   row of the Genre column.

2. Run the query. The Searchers is your movie.

The Or Operator

As you have seen, when we enter criteria in more than one column, Access assumes that we want to extract records that meet all the criteria in all the fields. Now suppose we have a movie-buff customer who wants to see a list of movies that are either Action or Horror. Follow these steps:

Using one field

1. Switch back to design view and delete the criteria under Date Released. Then replace the Genre criterion with *Action Or Horror*.

2. Run the query to extract the three movies that meet the criteria from the Movies table.

We can also use the Or operator with more than one field by using the Or row. Let's say the customer wants an action or horror movie, but also wants to see all the movies (regardless of genre) that are less than $40.00. Try this:

Using more than one field

1. Switch to design view and in the Or row of the Retail Price column, type *<40*.

2. Run the query. Now the datasheet shows all the movies that are either less than $40.00 or have a Genre value of Action or Horror.

The Not and Null Operators

We use the Not operator to identify the records that don't meet a specified criterion and the Null operator to identify the records that have no value in a specific field. For example, we can tell Access to identify all the movies in the Movies table that have a rating, like this:

1. Switch to design view and delete the criteria in the Retail Price and Genre columns.

2. In the Criteria row of the Rating column, type *Not none*. (Unlike in English class, double negatives are acceptable in database queries.)

Or rows

In the QBE grid, only one row is designated as the Or row. However, the Or operator is implied for all the rows below the Or row. If you need to use more Or criteria, enter them in successive rows.

3. Run the query. The datasheet shows only movies that have a rating other than NONE.

4. To save this query with a different name, simply choose Save As/Export from the File menu to display this dialog box:

Saving with a different name

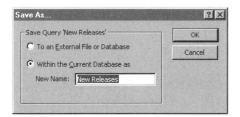

5. Type *Rated Movies* in the New Name edit box and click OK.

Sorting with Queries

A basic feature of databases is the ability to sort data so that we can look at it in different ways. For example, the Movies table is currently sorted in ascending order based on the primary key ID field. On page 21, we briefly mentioned that we can sort databases using the Sort Ascending and Sort Descending buttons. However, to sort on more than one column using this method, we have to rearrange the columns. Using a query, we can sort the table based on any criteria. For example, suppose we want to list the movies alphabetically by genre. Follow these steps:

1. Switch to design view and choose Clear Grid from the Edit menu to delete the fields from the QBE grid.

2. Double-click the Rating field in the Movies box to move the field onto the QBE grid, and then double-click Movie Name. (You may need to scroll to the left to see the fields on the QBE grid.)

3. Click the Sort row of the Rating column, click the arrow button, and select Ascending.

4. Repeat step 3 for the Movie Name field.

5. Run the query. The results are shown on the next page.

Exporting tables, forms, queries, and reports

Information from an Access database is often used as part of a report created in another program, such as Word or Excel. To export the data in a table, form, query, or report for use in another program, choose Save As/Export from the File menu, select the To An External File Or Database option, and click OK. Access then displays the Save In dialog box, where you can select a file format from the Save As Type dropdown list, name the file, and click Export. If you select Text Files as the format, Access displays the Export Text Wizard, which helps you set up the text file exactly as you want it. If you select Microsoft Access as the format, you must specify in the File Name edit box the database to which you want to export the table, form, query, or report.

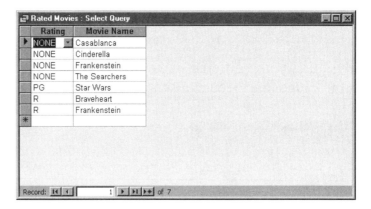

6. Close the query datasheet, clicking Yes to save your changes to the Rated Movies query.

With this introduction to queries under your belt, you are now equipped to carry out many of the queries commonly performed on databases. We'll pick up this topic later in Chapter 5, but for now let's move on to another tool for extracting information: reports.

Using Reports

Creating a report is similar to creating a form. We can create one quickly by using the default autoreport, or we can use the Report Wizard to produce results more tailored to our needs. And when a specialized report is required, we can customize reports using many of the same techniques we use for forms.

Creating AutoReports

To start exploring reports, let's create an autoreport based on the Movies table:

1. Close all open windows except the database window, and display the Tables tab.

2. Select Movies in the list of tables, click the arrow to the right of the New Object button on the toolbar, and select Auto-Report from the drop-down list. After a few seconds, Access displays the report shown on the facing page (we've scrolled the window so that you can see two records).

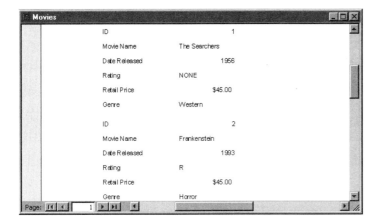

Because reports are usually created to produce printouts, Access displays the report in print preview so that you can see what it will look like on the page.

3. Click the Zoom button on the toolbar to zoom out for a bird's-eye view, like this:

The Zoom button

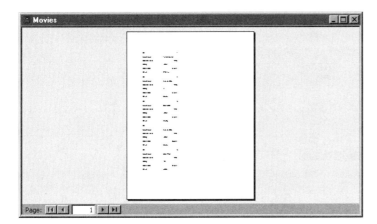

4. Click the Next Page button—to the right of the page indicator in the bottom left corner of the report window—to see the second page of the report. Then click the Zoom button again to zoom back in.

Creating Reports with the Report Wizard

You probably noticed that the records in the report are in ID order. Suppose we want them organized by rating order instead. To create a report that meets this need, we use the Report Wizard. Follow the steps on the next page.

1. Click the report window's Close button, and click No when Access asks whether you want to save the report.

2. In the database window, click the Reports tab and then click New to display this dialog box:

Selecting a table

3. Click Report Wizard, then click the arrow next to the Choose The Table Or Query edit box, select Movies from the drop-down list, and click OK to display the first Report Wizard dialog box:

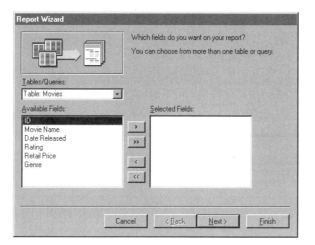

Other autoreports and wizards

From the New Report dialog box, you can choose to create two types of autoreports: Columnar creates labels and controls running down the side of the report, and Tabular creates an autoreport with labels and controls running across the top. We use the Chart Wizard on page 132 and describe the Label Wizard on page 78.

4. In this report, let's include all of the fields from the Movies table except the Movie ID. Click >> to move all the fields to the Selected Fields box, and then select ID and click < to remove it. Click Next to display the dialog box shown on the facing page.

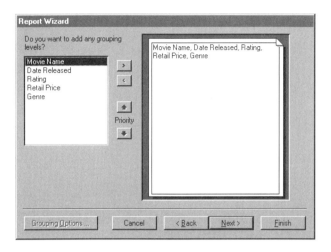

5. To specify a grouping level, you designate a field or fields that are to be used as the basis for organizing and sorting the report. Select Movie Name and click >. The preview on the right shows how the report will highlight the Movie Name field.

Grouping report fields

6. Now select Rating and click >. The dialog box now looks like this one:

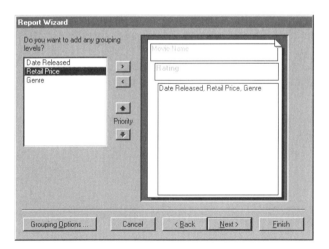

7. Since we really want to organize the list of movies by rating, the report should group by Rating first. To adjust the groupings, click the Movie Name field to highlight it in the preview window and click the down Priority arrow. After Rating and Movie Name switch places, click Next.

8. Access asks whether you want to sort the remaining fields in a given order. This table is too small to take advantage of this

Grouping by date or time

If you select a date field to group by when designing a report with the Report Wizard, Access gives you the option of grouping records by units of time from one minute up to a year. This can be useful when totaling sales for a month or quarter, or for almost any other time-dependent grouping of information.

option, but for larger databases you click arrows next to the edit boxes and select fields. In this case, simply click Next to display this dialog box:

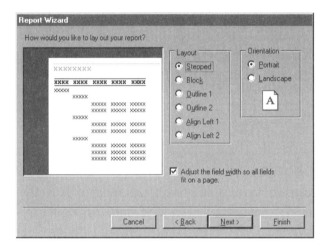

Changing sorting and grouping

Once you have assigned field groupings using the Report Wizard, you can change how the fields are sorted and grouped by switching to design view and clicking the Sorting And Grouping button on the toolbar. In the window that appears, you can add new fields for grouping, change the sorting for each field (ascending or descending order), and change the grouping order. (To move a field up or down in the grouping order, click the field's row selector, point to the selector, hold down the left mouse button, and drag up or down.) In the Group Properties section, you can assign headers and footers to each group, group by each value or by a prefix, group by an interval or number of characters, and tell Access whether to keep groups together across page breaks.

9. Select the various options and see the layout changes in the preview box on the left. When you've finished, select Outline 2 as the Layout option and Portrait as the Orientation option. Then click Next to move to the next dialog box:

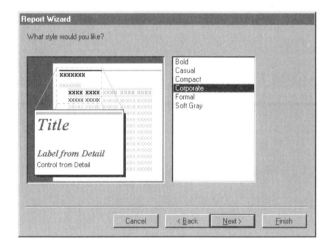

10. Try out the different styles, and when you have previewed them all, select Corporate and click Next.

11. Access suggests Movies as the title for the report. Accept this default name, leave the Preview The Report option selected, and click Finish to display the report in print preview, as shown here (again, we've scrolled the window):

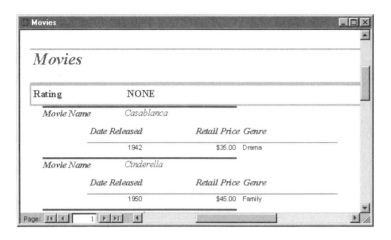

Modifying the Report's Design

The Report Wizard greatly simplifies the process of creating reports, and we can always modify a report's design later if it doesn't quite meet our needs. (The techniques we use are similar to those used to modify forms, so if you skimmed Chapter 2, you may want review the forms section.) Let's change the design of this report to enhance its appearance:

1. Switch to design view and, if necessary, close the Toolbox toolbar and click the Maximize button on the report window's title bar to expand the window like this:

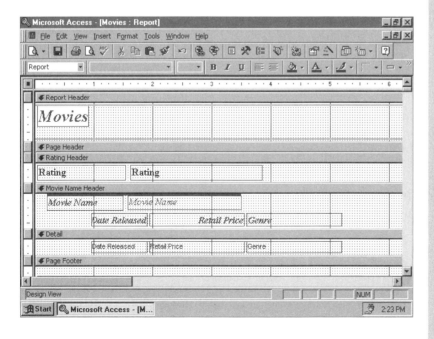

AutoFormats

If at any time you want to change the entire format of a report or form, you can use an autoformat. Switch to design view and click the report or form selector (the small box at the junction of the horizontal and vertical rulers) to select the entire report or form. (The box will contain a black square bullet.) Then click the Auto-Format button on the toolbar. Access gives you the same choices of formatting you had when using the Report or Form Wizard, including font, color, and border combinations. You can also create custom autoformats so that if you spend time working out the best layout for a report or form, you can easily repeat it.

This report is a good deal more complex than the forms you created in Chapter 2, but the major elements are the same. Controls placed in specific sections determine where the field values will be printed. The report's title, Movies, appears in the Report Header section and will be placed once at the beginning of the report. Rating has its own header, and the other fields have labels in the Movie Name Header section and controls in the Detail section. Also included are Footer sections for the page and for the report as a whole.

Deleting labels

2. When fields are fairly obvious, labeling them creates needless clutter on a report. Let's delete the labels for Rating and Movie Name. Select the Rating label (the box on the left) and press Delete. Repeat this step for the Movie Name label.

3. Now select the Rating control, point to its border, and when the pointer changes to an open hand, drag the control to the left.

4. Repeat step 3 to reposition the Movie Name control so that it aligns with the left end of the heavy line above, like this:

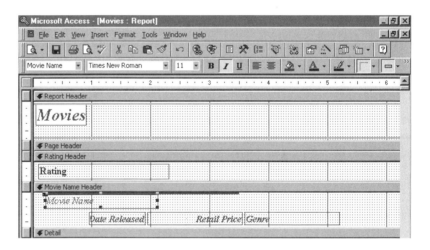

5. Now click the Print Preview button on the Report Design toolbar to see what the report looks like.

The Rating and Movie Name sections are now OK, but let's make the Detail section a little more presentable:

1. Switch to design view and click the Save button to safeguard the design changes you have made so far.

2. Now select all the labels in the Movie Name Header section (but not the Movie Name control) and all the controls in the Detail section. (Click one box, hold down the Shift key, and click each label and control to add it to the selection.)

3. Right-click any selected box and choose Properties from the object menu to display this dialog box, which lists all the properties used in reports:

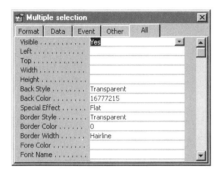

4. Scroll to the Text Align property (next to last on the All tab). Click the edit box, click the arrow button, and choose Center from the drop-down list. Close the Properties dialog box.

Aligning control and label text

5. Now move all of the selected labels and controls to the left to align with the Movie Name control.

6. Save the report and then click the Print Preview button to see how it is shaping up:

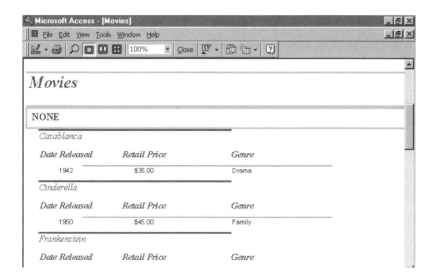

The Report Wizard added the gray boxes and blue lines to create visual structure in the report, but this formatting tends to clutter up the page. Let's trim it down a little bit:

Sizing sections →

1. Click Close on the Print Preview toolbar, and then enlarge the Rating Header section (point to the bottom of the section, and when the pointer changes to a bar with opposing arrows, drag downward).

2. Click the gray line below the Rating control to select it, press Delete, and shrink the Rating Header section again.

3. Select the thick blue line at the top of the Movie Name Header section and press Delete.

Aligning lines →

4. Now click the thin blue line above the controls in the Detail section. (It may be hard to spot at first, but look carefully.) When you have selected the line, hold down the Shift key and also select the Date Released control.

5. Choose Align and then Left from the Format menu to both move the line to the left and align it precisely with the Date Released control.

6. Now save and preview the report.

Not bad, but we could do a few more touch ups. The movie name should be bolder, and maybe we should have deleted the line between the Date Released, Retail Price, and Genre labels and their controls instead of the thick blue line between movies. Follow these steps to make these adjustments:

The Toolbox

We do not use many of the tools on the Toolbox toolbar, but a tool exists for almost every object you might want to add to a form or report. For example, you can use these tools to add text boxes, labels, option buttons, check boxes, graphics, and page breaks. Check online help for details about how to take advantage of these tools to customize forms or reports to meet your needs.

1. Close print preview, select the Movie Name control and click the Bold button. Then select the Date Released, Retail Price, and Genre labels and click the Bold button to turn off bold.

2. Point to the bottom of the Movie Name Header section, and when the pointer changes to a double-headed arrow, hold down the left mouse button and drag upward, shrinking the size of the Movie Name Header so that the labels just fit. (Access won't shrink the section beyond the bottom of the lowest label or control.)

3. Select the thin blue line in the Detail section and press Delete.

Now let's draw the thick blue line:

1. On the toolbar, click the Toolbox button to activate it. Then dock the Toolbox toolbar at the top of the window by double-clicking its title bar, so that you have an unrestricted view of the three labels in the Movie Name Header section.

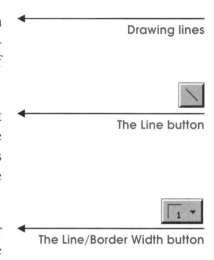

Drawing lines

The Line button

The Line/Border Width button

2. Click the Line button on the Toolbox, point to the top left corner of the Movie Name control, hold down the left mouse button, and drag to the right until the line spans the three labels at the bottom of the section. When you release the mouse button, the line snaps into place.

3. With the line selected, click the arrow next to the Line/Border Width button on the Formatting toolbar and select 3 from the drop-down list to change the thickness of the line to 3 pixels.

4. Click the arrow next to the Line/Border Color button on the Formatting toolbar and select dark blue.

5. Finally click the Properties button on the Report Design toolbar, set the Border Style property to Sparse Dots, and close the Properties dialog box.

6. Click the Toolbox button on the Report Design toolbar to toggle it off, then save, and preview the report, as shown here:

Adjusting lines

If you have difficulty drawing a straight line, use the Properties dialog box to fix the problem. The Height property indicates how far up or down a line slopes from its point of origin, not its length. To make the line straight, change the Height property to 0. To specify the exact length of a line, use the Width property. (Other types of controls also have Height and Width properties you can use to help with the precise placement or sizing of controls.)

Reports can become very complex and can include a good deal of formatting. We can't cover every technique for manipulating the appearance of reports, but you might take a look at some of the reports included with the sample databases that come with Access. For information about how to create reports based on multiple tables, see the tip on page 115.

Creating Mailing Labels

Now we'll take a quick detour to demonstrate another Access wizard: the Label Wizard. Once you learn how to use this wizard, you'll wish all programs made creating labels this easy.

Suppose Brock Buster's Video occasionally sends out promotions to all its customers. To save time, we want to create a mailing-label report that can be used to print a set of labels whenever they are needed. Follow these steps:

1. Close any open windows except the database window, and on the Reports tab, click New.

The Label Wizard ──────▶ 2. In the New Report dialog box, select Label Wizard, select Customers from the Choose The Table Or Query drop-down list, and click OK to display this dialog box:

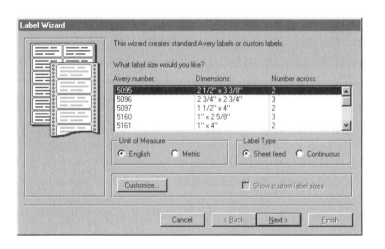

Using queries as a label source

You can use queries as the information source for labels. For example, to send information to customers in a specific sales area, you could create a query that extracts name and address information by city or Zip code and then use the query datasheet as the basis for a mailing-label report. You could also create product labels (videos, disks, and so on) this way.

3. Choose a label type (we chose Avery 5160) and click Next to display the dialog box shown at the top of the facing page.

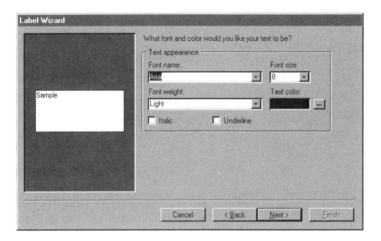

4. Change the font size to 10 and the font weight to Bold, and click Next to move to this dialog box:

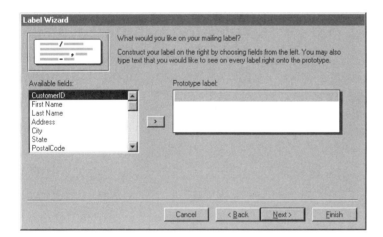

5. Double-click the First Name field to add it to the first line in the Prototype Label box, press the Spacebar to insert a space, double-click the Last Name field to add it after the space, and press Enter to create a second line.

6. Double-click the Address field, and then press Enter to create a third line.

7. Double-click the City field, type a comma and a space, double-click the State field, press the Spacebar twice, and then double-click the PostalCode field to finish the third line. Click Next to display the dialog box shown on the next page.

Adding fields

Avery labels

You will find almost all the Avery label formats listed in the Label Wizard's dialog box. If none of these label formats suits your needs, click the Customize button. In the dialog box that appears, click New. You can then specify the measurements of the label you want to use and save this new label for future use.

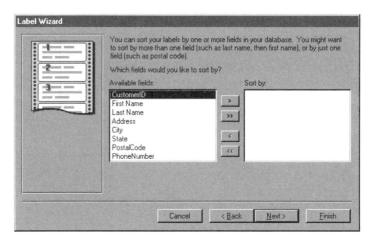

Sorting labels

8. Access allows you to sort the labels using any fields, even ones not included on the labels. For example, if you are doing a bulk mailing, you must sort by Zip code. For now, let's just sort by Last Name. Double-click Last Name and click Next.

9. Assign *Customer Mailing Labels* as the report's title and click Finish. Access displays the labels in print preview, as shown here (we've zoomed to 75% and scrolled the window to show all the labels):

Printing labels

Always print one test sheet of labels before sending an entire mailing-label report to your printer. To print just one page, choose Print from the File menu, select Pages in the Print Range section, type *1* in both the From and To boxes, and click OK. Then check the label alignment. If necessary, redo the mailing-label report by customizing the layout of your selected Avery label (see the tip on page 79) or by changing the font and font size. When you are sure the alignment is OK, print the entire mailing-label report.

Printing Reports

We have looked at reports in print preview several times to get an idea of how they will look when printed. Using print preview can save a lot of time and paper. If the report is too wide or too long to fit neatly on a page, print preview shows the overflow pages and allows us to change the report's design or modify the page setup before we commit it to paper. (We have covered several ways to change the report's design in this section; modifying the page setup was addressed briefly on page 24.)

Access has already set all the page setup options to print the mailing labels we created in the previous section, so we don't need to make any changes for this report. We can go right ahead and give the printer some work to do:

1. Click the Print button on the Print Preview toolbar to accept all print defaults. Or if you want to make any changes to the default print settings, choose Print from the File Menu.

2. Select the options you want, and click OK.

In this section, we have given you only a glimpse of the potential of Access reports, in the expectation that you will experiment with them as you use them. Remember, this experimentation has no effect on the structure of the underlying database tables or the data they contain.

Using Switchboards

A switchboard allows us to quickly access the most commonly used parts of the database. You may remember seeing the Northwind Traders switchboard when you opened that database in Chapter 1. To finish up this chapter, we'll show you how to create and customize a switchboard for the Brock Buster's Video database.

Creating a Simple Switchboard

At Brock Buster's Video, the most common tasks are entering new movies and entering new customers. Let's create a switchboard to quickly find those forms:

1. From any tab of the database window, choose Add-Ins and then Switchboard Manager from the Tools menu.

2. Click Yes when Access asks whether you want to create a switchboard. Access then displays the Switchboard Manager dialog box shown on the next page.

The OfficeLinks button

If you have Microsoft Office, it is simple to export the information in an Access table, query, or report for use in Word or Excel. Select the database component on the appropriate tab of the database window, click the arrow to the right of the OfficeLinks button on the toolbar, and select Publish It With MS Word or Analyze It With MS Excel from the drop-down list. The selected application opens with the table, query, or report loaded. You can also follow this procedure to use a table or query as a mail-merge data source, by clicking the arrow next to the OfficeLinks button, selecting Merge It With MS Word, and following instructions.

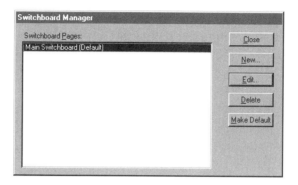

The switchboard is divided into pages, and usually the Main Switchboard is the first page we see when we open the database. Currently the switchboard is blank. Let's add the two forms we have already created to it:

Adding forms to a switchboard

1. Click Edit to display this dialog box:

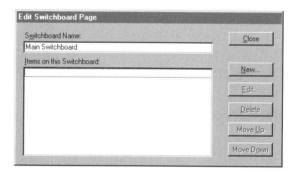

Setting the startup form

If you want to make a switchboard or any other form the first one seen when a database opens, choose Startup from the Tools menu and select the desired form name from the Display Form drop-down list. Other options in the Startup dialog box control whether toolbars can be customized, which object menus are available, and whether the database window and status bar are displayed. Any changes you make in this dialog box affect only the current database and will not take effect until you re-open the database or Access.

2. Click New to add an item to the Main Switchboard. Switchboard Manager displays this dialog box:

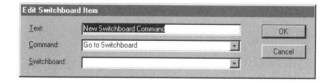

3. Type *Enter a new customer* in the Text edit box and select Open Form In Add Mode from the Command drop-down list. The Switchboard edit box becomes the Form edit box.

4. Select New Customers from the Form drop-down list and click OK to return to the Edit Switchboard Page dialog box, where Access has added *Enter a new customer* to the Items On This Switchboard list.

5. Repeat steps 2 and 3 to add an item that is linked to the New Movies form. Type *Enter a new movie* in the Text edit box, select Open Form In Add Mode as the Command setting, and New Movies as the Form setting.

Now let's see what the switchboard looks like:

1. Close the Edit Switchboard Page and Switchboard Manager dialog boxes.

2. If necessary, click the Forms tab in the database window. Then double-click Switchboard to display this window:

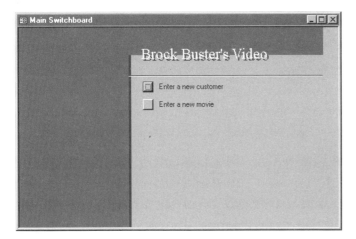

Customizing the Switchboard

As with reports, we can modify the format of a switchboard in many ways. Most of the rules for moving controls and labels in forms and reports also apply to switchboards. We won't spend a great deal of time adjusting this switchboard, but these steps will spruce it up:

1. Switch to design view.

2. Click in the colored area to the left of the grid to select the entire rectangle (handles appear around its borders), and press Delete to clear this area.

3. Now choose Picture from the Insert menu. Navigate to the Program Files\Microsoft Office\Office\Bitmaps\Dbwiz folder and double-click Videos. (We assume your Access picture files are stored in this default location. If they aren't, you may

Taking a shortcut to a database

Not only can you make the database start with an easy-to-use switchboard, you can make opening the database much easier. Shrink the Access program window so that the Windows 95 desktop is visible behind it, and then drag the switchboard form or any other database component out of the appropriate tab on the database window and onto the desktop. When you double-click the shortcut icon on the desktop, Access starts and the database is loaded with the selected component on the screen. To delete a shortcut icon, simply drag it to the Recycle Bin.

need to choose Find and then Files Or Folders from the Windows Start menu to locate the files.)

4. Switch to form view to see these results:

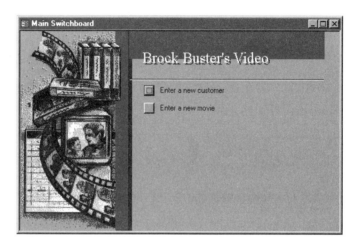

5. Click the switchboard window's Close button and click Yes when Access asks whether you want to save your changes.

Congratulations! You've now learned the basic skills needed to work with Access 97. In Part Two, we'll continue to use these tools, but we'll also cover some more complicated material and talk about database design.

PART TWO

BUILDING PROFICIENCY

In Part Two, we build on the techniques you learned in Part One to create an even more sophisticated database. After completing these chapters, you will be able to create and work with the main types of database components. In Chapter 4, we explore the important concepts of database design and how to create table relationships. In Chapter 5, we cover more complex combinations of forms and queries. In Chapter 6, we look at how to maintain databases by using action queries to manipulate multiple records, and how to secure databases by setting up groups, user accounts, and permissions for multiple users.

Database Design

4

Look up the possible
values for a field in
another table

Date	Customer	Video	Terms
6/1/97	1	1001	New Release
7/5/97	5	1002	New Release
6/15/97	1	1004	Oldie Weekend
7/15/97	3	1004	Oldie Weekend
7/1/97	2	1005	New Release

Create a One-To-Many
relationship directly
between two tables

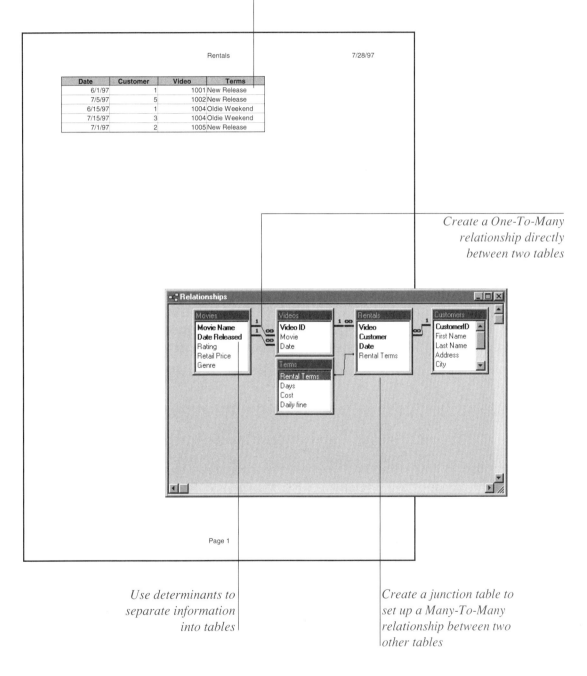

Use determinants to
separate information
into tables

Create a junction table to
set up a Many-To-Many
relationship between two
other tables

U p until now, we have created stand-alone database components using Access tools, but we haven't yet discussed how to create a relational database. Entire PhD theses have been written on the subject, but a few simple rules are all you need to keep most small to mid-size relational databases in shape. It's important to realize that although there are many ways to create a database, some ways are more efficient than others. You will need to balance added efficiency with expediency when deciding how much effort to put into designing your databases. The larger the database, the more important good design becomes.

Rules for Database Design

To understand the concepts behind database design and how it can help us create a more efficient storage tool, let's examine the Brock Buster's Video database we created in Part One of this book. The video store has customers and movies, and to keep track of them, we have already set up Customers and Movies tables. But we also want to keep track of rental transactions involving both customers and movies. Does that mean it would be best to keep customer and movie information in one big Transactions table?

Let's say for the sake of argument that we decide to create this Transactions table. When Jock Nicholson comes in to rent Braveheart, we enter a record containing this information:

Date	Name	Address	Phone	Movie	Price	Type	Rate
6/1/97	Jock Nicholson	123 Joker Street Hollywood CA 11403	(213)555-1111	Braveheart (1995)	$19.99	Drama/R	$3.50

Obviously such a table is cumbersome for several reasons:

- The table contains so much data that it's hard to isolate individual items of information. For example, finding PG-rated action movies from the 70s would be very difficult.

- Features such as list boxes and drop-down lists, which help speed up data entry, are not available because each field has too many possible entries.

- A lot of information is repeated. Each time Jock Nicholson rents a movie, we have to retype his name and address. Each time someone rents Braveheart, we have to retype the movie information. The database will grow rapidly as we store the same information over and over. In the database world, this is called *redundancy*.

Redundancy

- If we delete a record, we risk deleting information we want to save. For example, if Jock Nicholson moves to Seattle, we can't delete his records without destroying information about the movies he has rented. In the database world, this is called an *update anomaly*.

Update anomalies

- If Jock changes his phone number, we have to change it in every one of his records. Otherwise, someone might pull up the wrong information and call his old number. This is another example of an update anomaly.

Solving these problems is called *normalization*. We will not deal exhaustively with normalization, but we will give you three basic rules that will help you design your database in a way that avoids these problems.

Normalization

Rule 1: Keep Information Compartmentalized

To properly sort and retrieve information, we need to separate individual items of information and put them in different fields. This rule may seem obvious, but you'd be surprised how many people create Name fields like the example on the facing page and then realize later that they can't sort a table on people's last names. The example's Movie field also demonstrates the need for this rule. You might argue that using this field to find movies by the date of release would be easy using wildcards (see page 62), but the table would quickly become difficult to manage and could be corrupted by entries such as 1984 (1984) and 1941 (1979). So Rule 1 of database design requires that we separate the Name field into First Name and Last Name fields as we did in the Customers table of the Brock Buster's Video database, and that we separate the Movie field into Movie Name and Date Released fields as we did in the Movies table.

An exception to Rule 1
An exception to Rule 1 of database design is the date, which contains day, month, and year data and may seem cumbersome at first. However, using input masks, default values, and drop-down lists makes entering dates easy, and it is much easier to retrieve entire dates than to retrieve their component parts.

Rule 2: Separate Information Using Determinants

If we just worked with Rule 1, we could still create one big table containing all the information, and we would still have redundancy. The solution to this problem is to create separate, related tables. But how do we decide what information to spin off into a separate table?

Tables generally are designed around a kind of theme, such as movies, customers, or employees. In many cases, using our intuition about what should be in one table and what should be in another works just fine. But when intuition fails, we can fall back on Rule 2 of database design. The trick is to find one or more fields that determine the other fields. Database designers call this field or fields the *determinant*. The determinant then becomes the primary key for the table.

Determinants →

To find out if one field (X) is a determinant of another field (Y), ask this question: "If we know the value in field X, do we know the value in field Y?" For example, in a list of employees, we ask: "If we know the Social Security Number field value, do we know the First Name and Last Name field values?" The answer is "Yes" because every social security number is unique. Now let's look at a question from the Brock Buster's Video database: "If we know the Movie Name field value, do we know the Date Released, Rating, Price, and Genre field values?" If you think about it, the answer is "No" because we have two movies called Frankenstein. But suppose we modify the question to "If we know the Movie Name and Date Released field values, do we then know the Rating, Price, and Genre field values?" Then the answer would most likely be "Yes." So we can say that Movie Name and Date Released determine Rating, Price, and Genre.

Flat vs. relational databases

A flat database consists of a single, often very large, table from which you can extract individual items of information. But you can work only with the information in that one table. A relational database can have many tables; and fields in one table can be related to fields in other tables, enabling you to work with the information in all the tables.

Let's apply Rule 2 of database design to the Movies table of the Brock Buster's Video database, by deleting the ID field and designating the Movie Name and Date Released fields as the table's primary key:

1. Start Access, open the Brock Buster's Video database, and open the Movies table in design view.

2. Point to the primary key symbol in the ID field selector, and when the pointer changes to a right arrow, click to select the entire field. Then press Delete.

Deleting fields

3. When Access asks whether you want to permanently delete the field, click Yes. Click Yes again when Access warns you that the field is a primary key.

4. Now point to the selector for the Movie Name field, hold down the left mouse button, and drag downward until both the Movie Name and Date Released fields are selected.

Using multiple fields as the primary key

5. Click the Primary Key button on the toolbar. Here are the results:

The Primary Key button

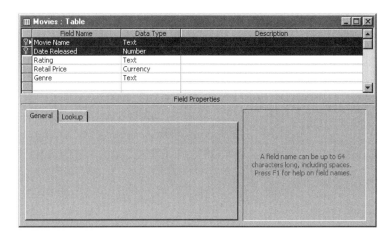

With these two fields as the primary key, Access won't allow two movies with the same name and release date in this table.

Now let's turn our attention to the Customers table. If we know a customer's first and last names, do we know the address? The answer is "Yes" for the customers we've entered so far. But what if we have two customers called John Smith? To account for this possibility, we would have to add a third field to come up with a determinant. In cases where we know that a set of information (in this case, about customers) should be in one table but the determinant is too complicated, it's best to let Access set the primary key by creating an AutoNumber field, or we can create a unique customer ID ourselves. (Why do you suppose every merchant you deal with gives you a new account number?)

Rule 3: Move Partial Dependencies to a Linked Table

Suppose Brock Buster's Video has 20 copies of Braveheart. How should we keep records for them? How do we know which copies have been rented and how many we have left? Our intuition may be to turn the Movies table into a Videos table that includes a Video ID field, like this:

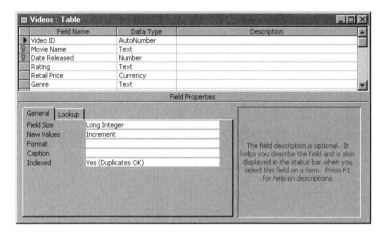

But there are several problems with this new Videos table:

- We would have to enter the Braveheart information 20 times instead of once.

- If the store acquired copies of the movie at different times, different employees might enter the Genre field value as Action, or even Horror, instead of Drama. Inadvertent errors like this one could mean quite a bit of repair work later.

Partially dependent fields

- This table has *partially dependent* fields. These are fields that are dependent on some of the other fields in the table but not all of them. Here, Rating, Price, and Genre are determined by Movie Name and Date Released, but not by Video ID.

Foreign keys

We can solve this type of problem by following Rule 3 of database design, which requires that we keep partially dependent fields in a table of their own and that we link their table to any related table using a *foreign key*. The foreign key then allows us to look up information in the related table instead of repeating it. This rule may require some trade-offs in efficiency vs. expediency. For example, we could create a comprehensive table of Zip codes and their corresponding cities and states. Then whenever a table contained address information, as the Customers table does, we could use a foreign key for the Zip field, omit the City and State fields, and have Access look up the city and state when needed. But for most databases, we would probably leave the partially dependent City and State fields and accept a little inefficiency rather than spend time creating the Zip table.

Efficiency vs. expediency

To apply Rule 3 to the Videos table shown on page 92, we need to think about movies and the way they are used in the video store. In reality, only one movie called Braveheart was released in 1995, but the store has several copies of it. We have movies, and we have copies of movies called videos. So what we need is one table for movies—the Movies table we have already created—and a separate table for videos—a new table that identifies all the copies of each movie. Isn't that redundant? No. Let's create the Videos table and see why:

1. With the Movies table open in design view and the Movie Name and Date Released fields selected, click the Copy button on the toolbar and close the Movies table, saving your changes.

Copying fields

2. Click New on the Tables tab of the database window, select Design View in the New Table dialog box, and click OK.

3. Call the first field *Video ID* and assign the Number data type. Click the Primary Key button on the toolbar.

4. Next, click the selector for the second field to highlight the entire field, and then click the Paste button on the toolbar. Access pastes in the definitions for the Movie Name and Date Released fields from the Movies table.

5. Now change the names of the second and third fields to *Movie* and *Date*.

6. Close the table, saving it as *Videos*.

We have now isolated the partially dependent fields. However, Access does not yet know that the Movie and Date fields in Videos are related to the Movie Name and Date Released fields in Movies. The copy-and-paste operation has transferred only the definitions of the fields. We need to establish a relationship between the two tables to let Access know that the data in these fields should correspond. Then if we need additional information about a video, such as its rating, Access can look in the Movies table to find it.

Establishing Relationships

We create relationships between tables so that we can combine the information from more than one table in queries, forms, and reports. A relationship is formed by matching the primary key field in one table with the foreign key field in another table. As you already know, the values in a primary key field must be unique. The values in a foreign key field need not be unique, but each one should match a value in the corresponding primary key field. Access provides a method called *referential integrity* to ensure that the field values match.

Referential integrity →

We can create these three types of relationships between two tables:

One-To-Many →

• One-To-Many, where a record that is unique in one table can have many corresponding records in the other table. For example, the value Braveheart occurs only once in the Movie Name field of the Movies table, but it can occur many times in the Movie field of the Videos table.

One-To-One →

• One-To-One, where a record that is unique in one table is also unique in the other table. This type of relationship is rare.

Many-To-Many →

• Many-To-Many, where a record that is unique in one table can have many corresponding records in the other table and vice versa. For example, each customer in the Customers table can rent many videos in the Videos table, and each video in the Videos table can be rented by many customers.

Don't worry if this sounds very confusing right now. In this section, we'll create a couple of One-To-Many relationships and a Many-To-Many relationship so that we can see how they work.

Creating a One-To-Many Relationship

Let's start by forging a relationship between the Movies and Videos tables so that Access will know that the data in the Movie Name and Date Released fields in Movies correspond with the data in the Movie and Date fields in Videos:

1. Click the Relationships button on the toolbar. Access opens the Relationships window and displays this dialog box:

The Relationships button

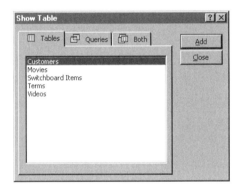

2. Double-click first Movies and then Videos to add these tables to the Relationships window, and then close the Show Table dialog box. (You may not be able to see the tables in the Relationships window until you close the Show Table dialog box.) The Relationships window looks like this:

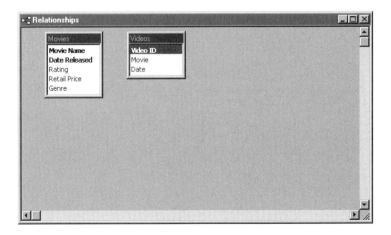

Defining the relationship

3. In the Movies box, select the Movie Name field, hold down the Shift key, and select the Date Released field.

4. Point to the selection, hold down the left mouse button, and drag to the Videos box. When you release the mouse button, the dialog box shown below appears:

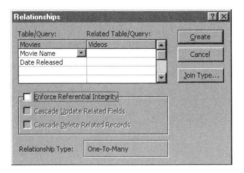

5. Click the first edit box under Videos in the Related Table/Query column, click the arrow button, and select Movie from the drop-down list.

6. Click the second edit box and select Date.

7. Next, click the Enforce Referential Integrity check box to turn on referential integrity. This step is essential if you want to reduce update anomalies and redundancy (see page 89). When this box is checked, Access won't allow you to enter Movie and Date values in the Videos table unless corresponding Movie Name and Date Released values exist in the Movies table. For example, if you try to enter *Brveheart* in the Movie field of the Videos table, Access will display an error message.

8. With Relationship Type set to One-To-Many to tell Access that each movie is listed once in the Movies table but can show up many times in the Videos table, click Create. Access closes the dialog box and indicates the new relationship as shown at the top of the facing page.

Join types

You will rarely use the Join Type button in the Relationships dialog box, but you may want to know what it does. You click this button when you want to tell Access how to use this relationship in queries. For those of you who are familiar with SQL, the available options represent Inner Join, Left Outer Join, and Right Outer Join, respectively. When Access runs a query using this relationship, the first option tells it to show only the records where fields from both tables match. The second option tells Access to show all the records in the first table and the matching records in the second table. And the third option tells Access to show all the records in the second table and the matching records in the first table.

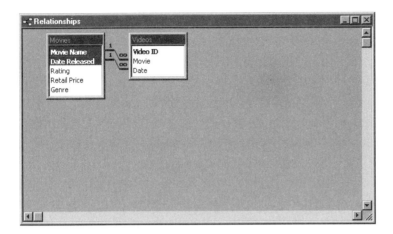

9. Close the Relationships window, clicking Yes to save the new relationship when prompted.

Now let's test the relationship by giving Brock Buster's Video store some inventory. Follow these steps to add records to the Videos table:

1. Open the Videos table and enter the following information:

Testing referential integrity

Video ID	Movie	Date
1000	Braveheart	1995
1001	Braveheart	1995
1002	Braveheart	1995
1003	Casablanca	1942
1004	Cinderella	1950
1005	Frankenstein	1993
1006	Gidget	1960

When you try to move to the next record after entering Gidget, Access displays this error message:

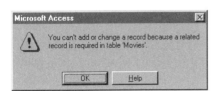

2. Click OK to close the message box, and then click the Undo button on the toolbar to clear the Gidget record.

The Undo button

3. Close the Videos table.

Creating a Many-To-Many Relationship

Now that we have a feel for relationships, we are ready to create the main relationship of the Brock Buster's Video database: between the Customers and Videos tables. This relationship is Many-To-Many because each customer can rent many videos and each video can be rented by many customers. We can't create a Many-To-Many relationship directly. Instead we must create a new table, called a *junction table*, that includes fields with the same definitions as the primary key fields from the two tables. We then set up One-To-Many relationships between each of the two tables and the junction table.

Junction tables

To create a Many-To-Many relationship between the Customers and Videos tables, we'll set up a junction table called *Rentals*. Follow these steps:

1. Click the arrow to the right of the New Object button on the toolbar and select Table from the drop-down list.

2. In the New Table dialog box, select Design View and click OK.

3. Define the following fields:

Field	Data Type	Field Properties
Video	Number	
Customer	Number	
Date	Date/Time	Format = Short Date

4. Select the Video, Customer, and Date fields and click the Primary Key button on the toolbar.

   Why do you need all three fields as the primary key? If you know the Video and Customer values, do you know the Date value? No, a customer might rent the same video on different days. If you know the Customer and Date values, do you know the Video value? Only if you restrict customers to one video a day. Do the Date and Video values tell you the Customer value? It's possible, but if someone rents a video in the morning and returns it in the afternoon, you can't rent the video again that day without corrupting the database. So you need all three fields to identify a unique rental transaction.

5. Close the table window, saving the table as *Rentals*.

Having created the junction table, let's create relationships with the Customers and Videos tables:

1. Click the Relationships button to display the Relationships window.

2. Click the Show Table button, and in the Show Table dialog box, double-click Customers and Rentals to add them to the Relationships window, and then close the Show Table dialog box. The Relationships window now looks like this:

The Show Table button

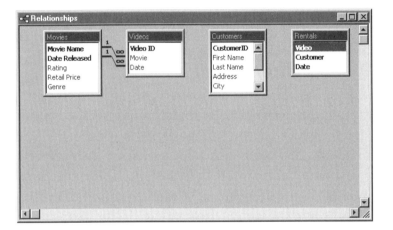

3. Rearrange the boxes so that the Rentals box sits between the Videos and Customers boxes. (Drag the box's title bar to move it.)

4. Now click the Video ID field in the Videos box and drag it over the Video field in the Rentals table. Access then displays the Relationships dialog box (as shown on page 96), where Video is already assigned under Rentals in the Related Table/-Query column.

5. Click the Enforce Referential Integrity check box and then click Create.

6. Repeat steps 4 and 5 to create a One-To-Many relationship by dragging Customer ID in the Customers table over Customer in the Rentals table. Access indicates the two new relationships as shown on the next page.

Cascading updates and deletions

Two additional options become available in the Relationships dialog box after you click the Enforce Referential Integrity check box. Click the Cascade Update Related Fields check box to tell Access to update corresponding values in a related table when changes are made to the primary key value in the primary table. (If the primary key field in your table is set to AutoNumber, clicking this option will have no effect since you can't change values in AutoNumber fields.) Click the Cascade Delete Related Records check box to tell Access that when you delete a record in the primary table, Access should delete any corresponding records in the related table. By turning on these options, you override the default settings, which prevent updating and deleting when the Enforce Referential Integrity option is checked.

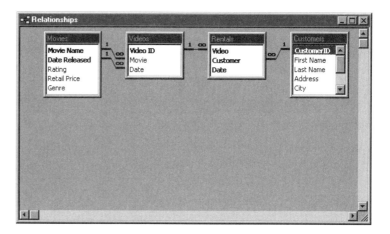

7. Close the Relationships window, saving your changes.

Creating a Relationship Using the Lookup Wizard

To make the Rentals table even more useful, let's include a field to hold the terms of each rental transaction. You may recall that the Brock Buster's Video database already includes a Terms table that spells out what terms are available. To ensure that only valid term data is used in the Rentals table, we can create a relationship between a Terms field in the Rentals table and the Rental Terms field of the Terms table. This time, we'll create the relationship using the Lookup Wizard. Follow these steps:

1. Open the Rentals table in design view and add a new field below Date called *Terms*.

2. In the Data Type column, click the arrow button and select Lookup Wizard from the drop-down list. The wizard displays its first dialog box (shown earlier on page 40).

3. With the option labeled *I want the lookup column to look up the values in a table or query* selected, click Next to display the dialog box shown at the top of the facing page.

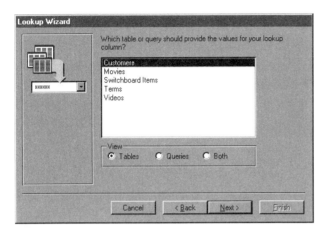

4. Double-click Terms to both select it and move to this dialog box:

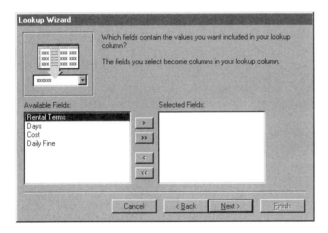

5. With Rental Terms selected, click the > button and then click Next to display this dialog box:

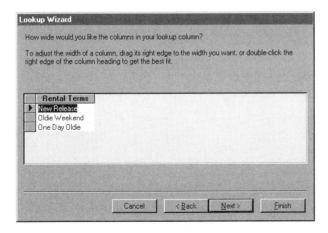

6. Click Finish and then click Yes to save the table and the new relationship. The design window now looks like this:

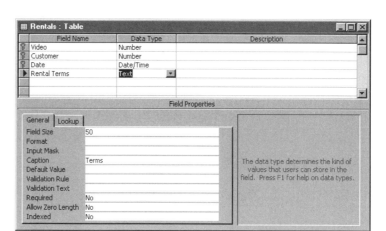

Notice that Access has changed the name of the new field to correspond with that of the Rental Terms field in the Terms table. The name you typed in step 1, Terms, is now the new field's caption.

7. With the Rental Terms field active, click the Lookup tab in the Field Properties section, and change the Limit To List property to Yes.

Let's take a look at the results of this procedure:

1. Switch to datasheet view, saving your changes to the table, click the Terms field in the first record, and click the arrow button. A drop-down list appears with the Rental Terms from the Terms table, like this:

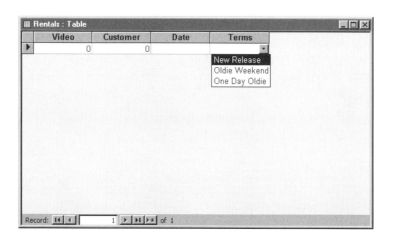

Changing or deleting relationships

Editing or deleting relationships is easy in Access. In the Relationships window, right-click the lighter middle part of the line indicating the relationship you want to change or delete. Then choose Edit Relationship or Delete from the object menu that appears. If you choose Edit Relationship, Access displays the Relationships dialog box (shown on page 96) so that you can make changes.

2. Close the table window, click the Relationships button to open the Relationships window, and enlarge the Rentals box so that you can see the new Rental Terms field. (Drag its bottom border downward.)

3. Click the Show Table button, and in the Show Table dialog box, double-click Terms to add it to the Relationships window. Then click Close. The Relationships window looks like this one:

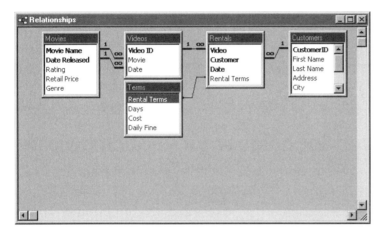

As you can see, the Lookup Wizard has created a relationship between the Terms and Rentals tables.

4. Close the Relationships window, saving your changes.

Let's take some time now to fine-tune the Rentals table and enter a few rental transactions, and then we'll move on to explore some of the tools Access provides for reducing errors:

1. Open the Rentals table in design view, where the fields are listed in the order in which you created them.

2. Rental transactions would logically be entered in date order, so click the selector for the Date field, point to the selector, and drag the selected field to the top of the field list. Then move the Customer field above the Video field.

Moving fields

3. Switch back to datasheet view, saving your changes.

4. Type *6/1/97* in the Date field, *1* in the Customer Field, *1001* in the Video field, and *New* in the Terms field. As soon as you

More about AutoCorrect

Some users appreciate Auto-Correct's assistance and others don't. AutoCorrect is turned on by default. To turn it off, choose AutoCorrect from the Tools menu and then deselect the Replace Text As You Type option. Other options at the top of the dialog box take care of common typing "errors." Access can correct two initial capital letters in a word, correct sentences that don't begin with a capital letter, capitalize the days of the week, and correct accidental usage of the Caps Lock Key. You can turn any of these options on or off by clicking the corresponding check box. If you click the Exceptions button, you can tell Access not to capitalize the word immediately following an abbreviated word (such as *apt.* for *apartment*). Or you can tell Access not to correct two consecutive initial capital letters in certain instances. If you find this feature useful, you can also use the AutoCorrect dialog box to assign your own shorthand words. For example, you might type *SS* in the Replace edit box, type *Steven Spielberg* in the With edit box, and click Add. Then you can type *SS* in a field, and Access will insert *Steven Spielberg* when you move to the next field. If you scan the list in the AutoCorrect dialog box, you will notice that AutoCorrect will also automatically fix several common spelling errors.

type the *N*, Access finds a match in the Rental Terms field of the Terms table and highlights it in the Terms field. You can then press Enter to move to the next record. This data entry shortcut is made possible by a feature called AutoCorrect. (Refer to the tip on this page for more information about AutoCorrect.)

5. Now enter these records:

Date	Customer	Video	Terms
6/15/97	1	1004	Oldie Weekend
7/1/97	2	1005	New Release
7/5/97	5	1002	New Release
7/15/97	3	1004	Oldie Weekend

6. Widen the Terms column so that you can see all the entries.

Design Techniques for Reducing Errors

You have already learned about several tools that help keep errors to a minimum, including primary keys, default values, input masks, combo/list boxes, and referential integrity. In this section, we will explore a few more tools that help us and the people who use our databases avoid mistakes.

Using Formulas as Default Values

In Chapter 1, we discussed using default values in the City, State, and Zip fields to save input effort and help avoid errors. We can also set a default value based on a formula to be calculated by Access. For example, in the Rentals table of the Brock Buster's Video database, we will rarely enter a date that is not the current date. People don't rent videos yesterday or tomorrow; they rent them today. So why not have Access enter the current date each time we make an entry? Follow these steps:

1. Switch the Rentals table to design view, click anywhere in the Date field, and click the Default Value edit box in the Field Properties section.

2. Click the Build button to the right of the edit box or click the Build button on the toolbar to display this dialog box:

The Build button

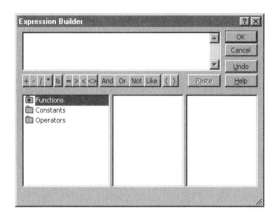

The *Expression Builder* is a very useful tool for manipulating data in Access. For example, you can use it to create formulas (equations) based on the values in other fields or on functions built into Access. The possibilities are virtually limitless. For now, we are going to use a simple function called *Date( )*, which pulls the date from your computer's built-in clock/-calendar and inserts it in the selected field.

The Expression Builder

3. Double-click the Functions folder and then click the Built-In Functions subfolder. Access displays categories of functions in the second list box and lists the functions in the selected category in the third list box.

Using built-in functions

4. Click Date/Time in the second box and double-click Date in the third box. The dialog box now looks like this:

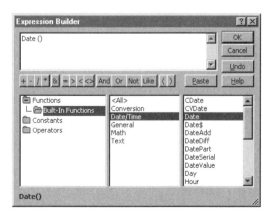

5. Click OK, and then close the table, saving your changes.

Other date/time functions

In addition to the Date() function, you can use other functions to work with date/time information. The two most common are Time(), which returns the time of day, and Now(), which returns the current date and time. If you want to explore other date/time functions, you can enter the name of the function in the Index tab of the Help Topics dialog box. For example, entering *DatePart function* and clicking Display gives you a full description of that function.

Now whenever a record is added to the Rentals table, the current date will appear by default.

Be careful to use formulas only when they are necessary. For example, you might be tempted to add a new field to the Rentals table called *Date Due* and to build a formula such as Date() + 1 as the field's default value. However, if you know the date the video was rented and the terms, you know the date due. There is no need to keep track of it because you can easily derive the date due from two pieces of information you already have. If you create a new field to store this information, you introduce redundancy, and after a few thousand rentals, your database will be bigger and slower than it needs to be.

Validation Rules

In Chapter 2's discussion of field properties, we skipped over the Validation Rule and Validation Text properties because it makes more sense to discuss them in the context of database design. When we set a validation rule for a field, Access allows only field values that meet the rule to be entered in the field. The kind of rule we can set up varies with the field's data type. We can specify that a text field should contain one of a set of values—for example, the City field should contain only Hollywood or Beverly Hills. We can specify that a date field should contain only the current date or a date that falls within a certain range. With number fields, we can specify that Access should accept only a specific value or a value that falls within a range. We can also specify that the values in a field must match the values in the same field in another table.

Let's look at an example. In the Movies table, the Date Released field has the Number data type. (We could have used the Date/Time data type, but we are interested only in the year, so why complicate things?) An employee could enter *1795* instead of *1975* in this field, and Access would accept it. To avoid this kind of data input error, we want the values in this field to fall between 1900 and, say, 2050. Follow these steps to create the necessary rule:

1. Open the Movies table in design view and click anywhere in the Date Released field.

2. Click the Validation Rule edit box in the Field Properties section, and then click the Build button to the right of the edit box. Access displays the Expression Builder dialog box shown earlier.

Building a validation formula

3. Click the > button, type *1900*, click the And button, click the < button, and type *2050*. Then if necessary, delete *Expr* and its enclosing chevrons, which Access may have inserted before the < symbol. The Expression Builder dialog box looks like this:

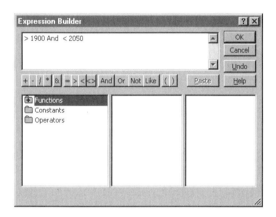

4. Click OK to close the dialog box and to enter the formula in the Validation Rule edit box.

5. Click the Validation Text edit box, and type *Value must be between 1900 and 2050*. Access will display this message whenever an unacceptable value is entered.

Adding validation text

6. Switch to datasheet view, save the changes to the table's structure, and click Yes when Access asks whether you want it to test existing data in the Date Released field against the new validation rule.

Now for the acid test:

1. Change the Date Released field value for Cinderella to *11*, and then try moving to another record. Access displays the message box shown on the next page.

2. Click OK in the message box and press the Esc key to restore the original value in the Date Released field.

3. Close the table window.

As you can see, validation rules are powerful tools that can help us ensure the accuracy of our data. The need for a validation rule may not be apparent when you first create a table; you may identify the need only after problems begin to show up. So it's good to know that you can always go back and add these safeguards later.

Protecting Your Data

If you are running Access on your own computer at work or at home, you probably don't have to worry about the kinds of conflicts that can arise when more than one person has access to the same database. However, if you share a computer, you might have concerns about protecting your data, and if you work on a network, protecting your data becomes a necessity. We can lock a record or an entire database to temporarily control access, and we can create passwords to control access more permanently. We talk about security and passwords in Chapter 6. Here we'll take a quick look at the temporary protection methods.

Unlike many applications that wait for us to tell them when to save information, Access saves the values in a new or edited record as soon as we move to another record. As a result, two or more people on a network can work on the same table at the same time. To prevent someone else from working on the record we are working on, we can lock the record, like this:

Backing up

Regularly backing up your files is an important aspect of database security. In addition to copying your database files to disks or tape for storage away from your computer, you might want to create a Backup folder in which you can store a copy of your working files to protect against inadvertent changes.

1. Choose Options from the Tools menu to display the Options dialog box, and then click the Advanced tab to display the options shown on the facing page.

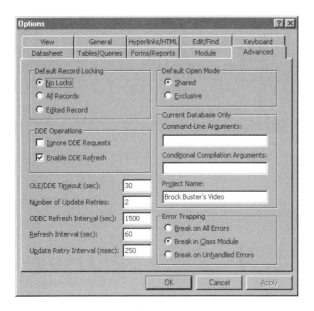

Notice the three options in the Default Record Locking section. No Locks is the default. The Edited Record option locks the record that is being edited in a table, form, or query and is appropriate for when you only occasionally have two or more people working on the same database at the same time. The All Records option not only locks all of the records in an open table, form, or query, it also locks all related tables. All Records is the most conservative option, because it can have the effect of locking the entire database file until you close it. It is the best option if several people often work on the same database and data integrity is a very high priority.

2. We won't apply any locks at this time, so click Cancel to close the Options dialog box.

You've learned a good deal about database design in this chapter, and some of the concepts may seem confusing. If it's any consolation, few people can set up a database correctly right off the bat. You should always play around with dummy data to start with, so that you can go back and change things until you get them right. It can be frustrating, it can be a challenge, and once in a while, it's even fun!

Sample databases

Access 97 includes many more sample databases than previous versions. You can use individual tables as the basis for those in your own databases, as we did in our example (see page 11). Or you can use the entire database, complete with tables, forms, queries, reports, and switchboards, and then customize the database to meet your own needs. You can also study the sample databases to get ideas about how to construct databases. On the Databases tab of the New dialog box, double-click any database icon, and Access will guide you through its construction.

5

More Sophisticated Forms and Queries

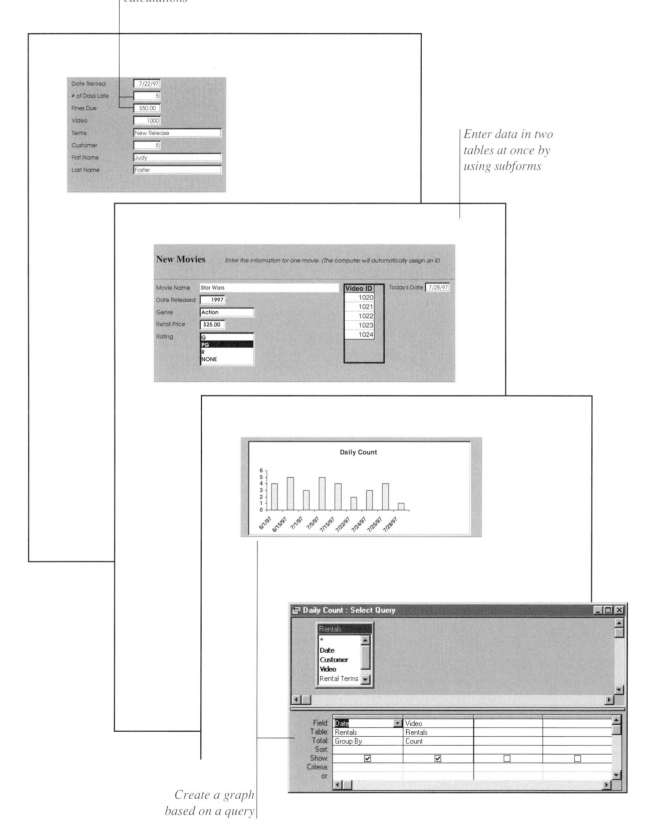

*Use unbound controls
in a form to perform
calculations*

Date Rented	7/22/97
# of Days Late	5
Fines Due	$50.00
Video	1000
Terms	New Release
Customer	5
First Name	Judy
Last Name	Foster

*Enter data in two
tables at once by
using subforms*

New Movies *Enter the information for one movie. (The computer will automatically assign an ID*

Movie Name	Star Wars
Date Released	1997
Genre	Action
Retail Price	$25.00
Rating	G / PG / R / NONE

Video ID
1020
1021
1022
1023
1024

Today's Date 7/28/97

Daily Count

6/1/97 6/15/97 7/1/97 7/5/97 7/15/97 7/22/97 7/24/97 7/25/97 7/28/97

*Create a graph
based on a query*

Daily Count : Select Query

Rentals
*
Date
Customer
Video
Rental Terms

Field:	Date	Video		
Table:	Rentals	Rentals		
Total:	Group By	Count		
Sort:				
Show:	☑	☑	☐	☐
Criteria:				
or:				

I n Part One, we created forms and queries that worked with the data in single tables and used very simple functions. In this chapter, we'll see how forms and queries can work with several tables and can include complex functions that make a database easier to use. As you learned in Chapter 4, good database design tends to increase the number of tables in a database, which in turn increases the number of relationships and primary and foreign keys that you have to deal with. To avoid confusion, we can use forms and queries to create an intuitive interface that requires no knowledge of the underlying structure of the database. We'll look at both forms and queries here, starting with forms.

Creating Multi-Table Forms

As you know, forms are a useful way of entering or editing data in a single table, but we can also use forms to view, add, or edit data in multiple tables. That's what makes them so powerful. Someone can enter information in just one form, and behind the scenes, Access will shuffle the individual items into their designated tables.

Forms and relationships

When we create a form based on two or more tables, we can take advantage of any existing relationships. Access traces the relationships through as many tables as necessary to find the correct information. As a demonstration, let's create a form for entering new rental transactions in the Brock Buster's Video database. In addition to showing all the fields in the Rentals table, it will show the customer's name (from the Customers table), the movie name (from the Videos table), and the movie rating (from the Movies table). Follow these steps:

1. Start Access and open the Brock Buster's Video database.

2. Create a new form using the Form Wizard.

Specifying multiple tables

3. Select Table: Rentals from the Tables/Queries drop-down list and move all its fields to the Selected Fields box. Then select Table: Videos from the drop-down list and move Movie to the

Selected Fields box. Select Table: Movies and move Rating. And finally, select Table: Customers and move First Name and Last Name. Then click Next.

4. In the next few dialog boxes, leave By Rentals as the viewing option, Columnar as the layout option, Standard as the style option, and Rentals as the form's title. Click Finish to display the form, which looks like this:

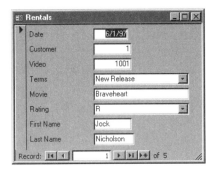

The record for the first video rental appears in the first four fields, followed by the information from the Videos, Movies, and Customers tables.

Did you notice that we have a problem waiting to happen with this form? As things stand, someone could tab down to the First Name field and change it to *Bob*. Because this form is intended to be used to enter rentals, not edit movie information or customer names, we should not only make the Movie Rating, First Name, and Last Name fields unavailable, but also make it clear on the form that the user shouldn't even try to change them. Follow these steps:

1. Switch to design view, maximize the form window, and if necessary close the Toolbox.

2. Increase the size of the Detail section's grid, delete some labels and adjust the size of others, and then move the controls so that your form looks like the one shown on the next page. (If you need a refresher on sizing and moving labels and controls, refer to Chapter 3, page 74.)

The trouble with wizards

Wizards are powerful tools that help you accomplish many tasks. But if you create objects using wizards and then try to go back and modify them, you may run into error messages you do not understand. Often it's easier to go back and recreate the object rather than modify a wizard-created one.

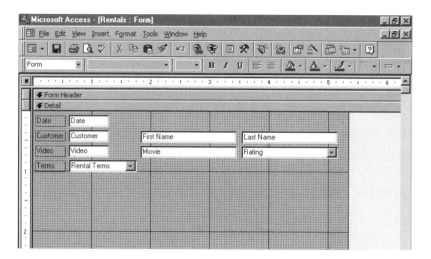

3. You don't want the Rating value to be changed in this form, and leaving the Rating control as a combo box is too tempting. Right-click the control and choose Change To and then Text Box from the object menu.

Disabling fields

4. With the Rating control still selected, hold down the Shift key and click the First Name, Last Name, and Movie controls to add them to the selection. Then right-click one of the selected controls, choose Properties from the object menu, change the Enabled property to No, and close the Properties dialog box. Access changes the background color of the selected controls and dims the text. (You can't customize either of these control elements, but you can change the border color.)

Setting forms for new data entry only

5. Finally, double-click the form selector at the junction of the horizontal and vertical rulers, to display the Properties dialog box for the entire form. Then change the Data Entry property to Yes and close the dialog box.

6. Now save the form.

By changing the form's Data Entry property, we specify that the form should be used only for creating new entries. We cannot scroll back through existing rentals. Let's add some more rentals now to see how the form reacts:

1. Switch to form view, where the new form looks like this:

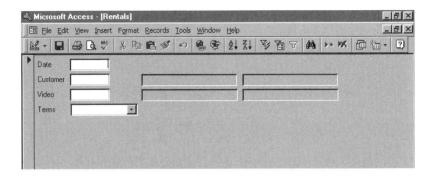

2. Enter the following rental transactions:

Date	Customer ID	Video	Terms
7/22/97	5	1004	Oldie Weekend
7/24/97	5	1005	One Day Oldie
7/25/97	2	1002	New Release
7/28/97	3	1001	New Release

3. Close the Rentals form.

4. Just to confirm that the form has done its job, open the Rentals table, which contains four new records, and then close it.

Adding Subforms

Sometimes we'll want to enter information in two or more related tables using one form. The best format for achieving this level of efficiency is a main form with one or more subforms. For example, we currently enter a new movie record in the Movies table and then enter the video records for that movie in the Videos table. It may seem like a lot of work to open one form and enter a movie, and then open another form and repeat some of the same information to record each video. Because these two tables are related, we can use a main form with a subform to make the process more efficient. We already created a New Movies form in Chapter 2 (see pages 43-45), so now we need to create another form that we can use as a subform. Follow these steps:

1. First use the Form Wizard to create a new form based on the Videos table. Move only the Video ID field to the Selected Fields box and then click Finish to accept all of the wizard's default settings.

Reports based on multiple tables

Reports sometimes contain information from more than one table. (They can also be based on multiple queries.) For example, if Mr. and Mrs. Buster want to see which customers are renting which movies on a monthly basis, the report must contain information from the Customers table and the Rentals table. First create two reports, one containing customer information and the other containing rental information. Then open the Customers report in design view, click the Subform/Subreport button on the Toolbox toolbar, and draw a subreport control in the Detail section. The Subreport Wizard walks you through the process of identifying the source report and the fields you want to include in the subreport. You can reformat the resulting subreport to suit your needs.

2. Switch to design view, where the form looks like this:

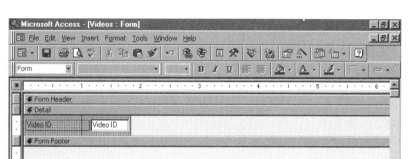

Specifying the default view

3. Double-click the form selector to display the Properties dialog box, change the Default View setting to Datasheet, and close the dialog box.

4. Close the form, saving your changes.

Now we need to tell Access that the Videos form is a subform of the New Movies form. Here's how:

1. Open the New Movies form in design view.

2. Earlier, you deleted the Movie ID field from the Movies table (the basis for this form), so go ahead and delete both the ID control and its label.

3. Now move and resize the controls and their labels so that they appear like this:

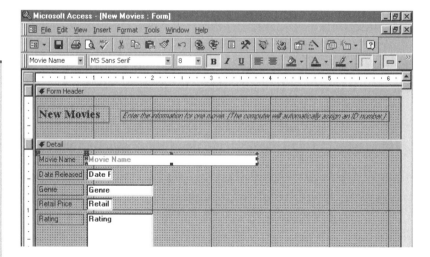

Handy helpers

To save time as you work on the design of a form, you can open the Properties dialog box, Toolbox toolbar, and Field List window and leave them open while you switch between form view and design view. All three of these tools disappear but stay active when you switch to form view and then reappear as soon as you switch back to design view.

4. Click the Toolbox button on the toolbar to display its toolbar, and then click the Subform/Subreport button.

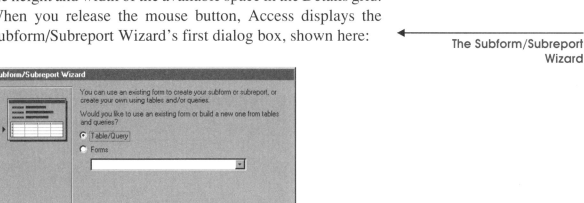

The Subform/Subreport button

5. Move the subform pointer to the right of the Movie Name control, hold down the left mouse button, and drag a frame the height and width of the available space in the Details grid. When you release the mouse button, Access displays the Subform/Subreport Wizard's first dialog box, shown here:

The Subform/Subreport Wizard

6. Click the Forms option, select Videos from the drop-down list below, and click Next to display this dialog box:

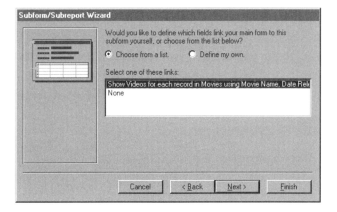

7. Access has identified the relationship between the two tables and knows how to link them, so click Finish.

8. Back in design view, click the arrow to the right of the Object box at the left end of the Formatting toolbar, scroll the list of form elements, and select Videos Label to select the label above and behind the Videos subform control. Then press the Delete key to delete the label.

The Object box

The Object box, located to the left of the Font box on the Formatting toolbar, is a handy feature for working with reports or forms whose objects are not all in view. You can click the box's arrow and select any object on the current form or report from the drop-down list. The object is then highlighted on the form or report, and its name is displayed in the Object box.

Sizing subforms

9. Drag the bottom center handle of the subform control down to enlarge the control so that it aligns with the Rating control.

10. Then double-click the form selector, change the Data Entry property in the Properties dialog box to Yes so that we can enter new videos but not edit existing ones, and close the dialog box.

11. Switch to form view, where the New Movies form now looks like this:

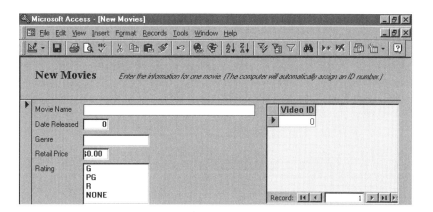

And there we have it! Suppose a new shipment of videos arrives at Brock Buster's Video—say five copies of Tin Cup. Let's see the form in action:

Testing the form

1. Tab through the form to see how smoothly the information can be entered into both the New Movies form and the Videos subform.

2. Enter the following information:

Movie Name	Date Released	Genre	Retail Price	Rating
Tin Cup	1996	Comedy	$19.99	PG

3. Now enter five Video ID values from 1006 to 1010.

Verifying data entry

4. Close the New Movies form, saving your design, and then open the Movies and Videos tables in turn to verify that the data you entered in the form has been transferred to the tables.

By now, you are probably beginning to see how good database design and well-thought-out forms can make data entry easy and efficient.

Adding Command Buttons

One of the most useful tools we can add to a form is a command button. Command buttons allow us to switch to a different form, search for specific records, exit the database, and perform a whole host of other tasks. As an example, we'll create a Find button on the New Customers form, so that when we need to change a customer's address or phone number, we can easily search for the correct record. Here are the steps:

1. Open the New Customers form in design view and then click the Command Button button on the Toolbox toolbar.

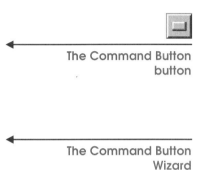

The Command Button button

2. Move the pointer to the right of the First Name control, hold down the left mouse button, and drag to create a small box. When you release the mouse button, Access displays the Command Button Wizard's first dialog box:

The Command Button Wizard

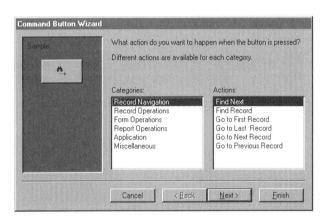

3. Select Record Navigation in the Categories list, select Find Record in the Actions list, and click Next to display the second dialog box:

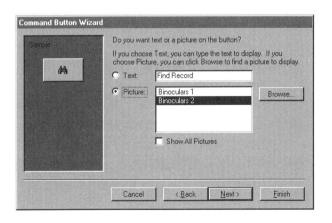

Other command button actions

In the Command Button Wizard's first dialog box , be sure to check in the Categories list to get an idea of the range of actions for which you can create command buttons. Most of the actions are self-explanatory, because they are basic functions of the program.

4. With the Picture option and Binoculars 2 selected, click Next to display this dialog box:

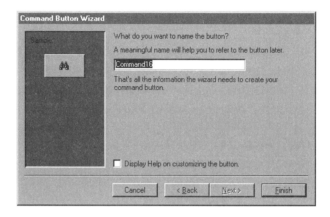

5. In this last dialog box, type *Find Customer* as the name of the button, and click Finish. Here's the result:

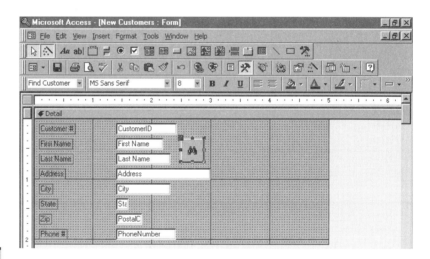

Other ways to identify command buttons

In the Command Button Wizard's second dialog box, Access displays a list of the pictures corresponding with the action you have chosen. But you are not limited to this list. You can click Show All Pictures to list all available pictures, and you can click the Browse button and navigate to a particular bitmap file you want to use.

Notice that Access automatically resized the button to fit the graphic you chose in step 4, and that because the button is still selected, its name (Find Customer) appears in the Object box at the left end of the Formatting toolbar.

6. Click the Save button to save the changes to the form.

Now for the acid test. Let's try out the new button:

1. Click the View button on the toolbar to switch to form view, and then click the form's new Find Customer button. Access displays this Find dialog box:

2. Type *5* in the Find What edit box and click Find First. Access displays the record for Judy Foster, whose Customer # field value is 005. You can now make any necessary record changes.

3. Click the Close button to close the dialog box, and then close the form.

   The ability to create buttons to perform routine actions really enhances what we can do with forms. (If you are interested in programming, you can also create your own actions with Visual Basic and launch them by clicking command buttons. This topic is beyond the scope of this book, but to find out more you can check the Visual Basic topics in Access's online help.)

   ◄ **Visual Basic**

Adding the Date

With controls, we can display all sorts of information in a form—some from tables or queries and some from other sources. For example, we can display the current date in the New Movies form by following these steps:

1. Open the New Movies form in design view and decrease the width of the Videos subform control to about 7/8 inch.

◄ **The Text Box button**

2. Click the Text Box button on the Toolbox toolbar, and create a text-box control about 1/2 inch wide to the right of the Videos subform control. The new control is designated as Unbound because it is not linked to any table, and it has a label identifying it as a text control. (If the label is hidden behind the Videos control, move the new control to the right until you can see it.)

   ### ControlTips

   By now you are probably familiar with the ToolTips feature of most Windows applications. You can create similar tips within your database to help the user. Simply type in the ControlTip Text edit box of the Properties dialog box whatever information you want displayed. In form view, this text will appear when the pointer pauses over the control.

3. Click the new control (the word *Unbound* disappears), type =*Date( )*, and press Enter.

4. Point to the control's border and double-click to display its Properties dialog box. Set the Format property to Short Date and close the dialog box.

5. Click the Text label, type *Today's Date:*, and press Enter. Then adjust the label's size, and reposition the form's elements as necessary to make everything fit.

6. Click the View button on the toolbar to see these results:

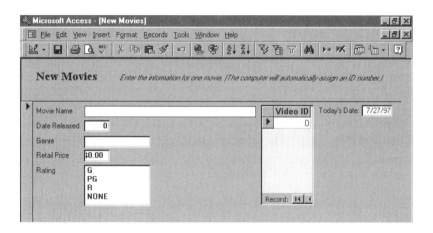

7. Close the form, saving your changes.

Adding the time and page number

You could also create controls to show the time (*=Time()*) and page number (*=Page()*).

Using Queries and Forms Together

Using queries and forms together provides a greater degree of flexibility than working with just one or the other. In this section, we'll show you several ways in which you can combine queries and forms to accomplish specific tasks. Bear in mind that our examples can easily be adapted and extended to meet the needs of your own databases.

Using Parameter Queries with Forms

Parameter queries take the work out of locating specific records. Of course, we could open the appropriate table and use the Find command or a filter to do our searching, but these tools take several steps and can be confusing to uninitiated users. Once we have set up a parameter query, simply opening the query displays a dialog box where we enter the record we are looking for. Access then displays that record

What is a parameter?

Programmers and mathematicians know what a parameter is, but the word may be unfamiliar to many users. Think of a parameter as being similar to the criteria you enter in the Criteria row of the QBE grid. It is a piece of information that Access needs in order to be able to carry out a specific task. In our sample parameter query, the parameter you enter identifies the record you are looking for.

in a datasheet. As you'll see, we can also combine a parameter query and a form to display the record in a form instead.

Let's say we want to create a form for one of the most basic tasks in the video store: logging in returned videos. For this form all we really need are a Video ID field and a new field to record that the video has been returned. Follow these steps to create a new field called *Returned?* in the Rentals table:

1. Open the Rentals table in design view, add a field called *Returned?*, set its data type to Yes/No, and switch to datasheet view, saving your changes. Notice that Access has put check boxes in the Returned? field. An unchecked box represents a No field value, and a checked box represents a Yes field value.

   The Yes/No data type

2. In the table, click the Returned? check box for all but the latest transaction for each video. (Obviously, a video must be returned before it can be rented again.)

   With this preparation out of the way, we can set up a parameter query for returned videos. Follow these steps:

1. Click the arrow to the right of the New Object button on the toolbar, select Query from the drop-down list, and with Design View selected in the New Query dialog box, click OK.

2. The Rentals box should be displayed in the query window. If it's not, double-click Rentals in the Show Table dialog box, and then click Close.

3. Double-click the Video and the Returned? fields to add them to the QBE grid.

4. In the Criteria row of the Video column, type *[Enter the video ID number]*. Enclosing the instruction in square brackets tells Access to display the instruction in a dialog box so that you can specify the video you are looking for.

5. In the Criteria row of the Returned? column, type *No*. The query window now looks like the one shown on the next page. (We widened the first column to display all of the instructional text.)

Quick table addition

You can quickly add a table to the query window by dragging the table's name from the database window to the query window. Access displays a box with all the table's field names, just as if you had used the Show Table dialog box to add the table.

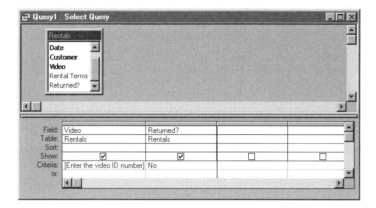

6. Close the query, saving it as *Returned Videos*.

Now let's create a form based on the query:

Basing a form on a query

1. With Returned Videos selected on the Queries tab of the database window, click the New Object button's arrow and select AutoForm from the drop-down list. Access displays this dialog box:

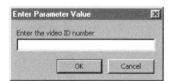

2. Type *1001* and press Enter. Access closes the dialog box and displays an autoform based on the Returned Videos query, like this (we clicked the Restore button at the right end of the title bar to shrink the size of the form window):

3. Click the Returned? check box and close the form window, saving the form as *Returned Videos*.

4. Now check the Rentals table to be sure that the return information was processed correctly through the Returned Videos query, like this:

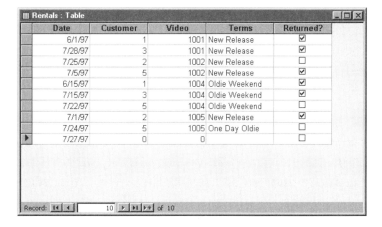

5. Close the table.

Using Formulas in Queries

Multi-table queries can be useful for accessing fields so that they can then be used in calculations. As you'll see, when we want to use the value of a field in a calculation, we simply enclose the field name in square brackets.

Let's say, for example, that we want to create a form that finds all customers with late videos, displays how late they are, and calculates the fine they owe. The Rentals table doesn't have a field called *Number of Days Late* but it contains the information necessary to calculate this value. First, follow these steps to create a query that combines all the necessary fields:

1. With Rentals selected on the Tables tab of the database window, select Query from the New Object drop-down list on the toolbar and click OK to open the query in design view, where Rentals has already been added to the query window.

2. Click the Show Table button on the toolbar and add the Customers and Terms tables to the query window. Three tables are now available.

3. Move all the fields from the Rentals table to the QBE grid. Then scroll the grid, move First Name and Last Name from Customers, and move Days and Daily Fine from Terms.

4. In the Criteria row of the Returned? column, type *No* to identify the videos that have not been returned.

Using field values in calculations

Relating tables

You can relate two tables that do not have a previously defined relationship in the query window. Click and drag from the linking field in the first table box to the linking field in the second table box. Access draws a line between the two fields. Remember, the fields must contain corresponding values for the two tables to be related. To dissolve a relationship, click the line between the two table boxes to select it, and then press the Delete key. Relationships defined in a query window will not be reflected in the Relationships window—they exist for that query only.

5. In the Criteria row of the Date column, type <(*Date( )-[Days]*). You are telling Access to calculate whether today's date minus the number of days in the rental period (the value in the Days field) is greater than the date on which the video was rented. If it is, the video is overdue.

In a real database, this query would be reusable because Access adjusts the criteria using the *Date( )* command each time we run the query. Before we can test the query on the sample database and see any results, however, we need to change the criteria so that the query will work with our fabricated dates. Here's how to test the query:

1. Change *Date( )* in the Criteria row of the Date column to *#7/28/97#* (the # symbols let Access know that this is a date format), so that the criteria is <(#7/28/97#-[Days]).

2. Now run the query. Access identifies these overdue videos:

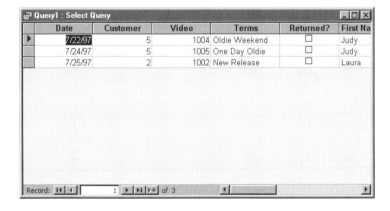

3. Close the query, saving it as *Late Videos*.

Using Calculated Controls in Forms

We now have half of the job accomplished; we have found the overdue videos, but we have not yet calculated the fines. To complete the job, we need to create a form with some calculated controls. Follow these steps:

1. With Late Videos selected on the Queries tab of the database window, select AutoForm from the New Object drop-down list, switch to design view, and maximize the window.

Adding a group of option buttons

Option buttons and check boxes should be familiar by now, but the difference between them may not be readily apparent. In the Print dialog box, for example, you see round option buttons in the Print Range section for All, Pages, or Selected Records. You must choose one and only one of these option buttons to be able to print. The check boxes, Collate and Print To File, can be selected singly, together, or not at all. You can add a group of option buttons to a form by clicking the Option Group button on the Toolbox toolbar. After you draw a box in the desired area, Access displays the first Option Group Wizard dialog box. Here, you list the options in the group. Then indicate whether one option is the default and if so, which one. Next, specify the values to be assigned to each option for storage purposes and where you want the value stored. Then specify how the buttons should look on the form, and assign them a group name. On the form, the buttons appear surrounded by a group box, and only one can be selected at a time. Similarly, you can add check boxes to a form by clicking the Check Box button on the Toolbox toolbar.

2. Rearrange the labels and controls on the form so that it looks like this:

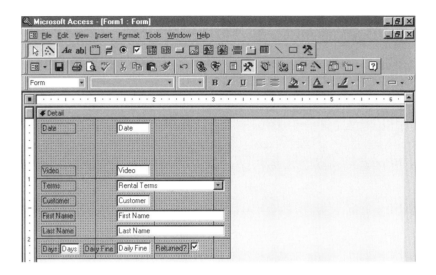

We don't really need the three fields at the bottom of this form, but having them available makes it easier to construct the calculations we need. So instead of deleting them, let's make them invisible:

1. Select the labels and controls for Days, Daily Fine, and Returned? by holding down the Shift key and clicking each one. Click the Properties button on the toolbar, change the Visible property to No, and close the dialog box. (The labels and controls are invisible only in form view.)

Making fields invisible

2. Click the Text Box button on the Toolbox toolbar and insert an unbound text control just below the Date control. Repeat this step to insert another text control just below this one.

3. Now click the Date label, click the Properties button, change its Caption property to *Date Rented*, and close the Properties dialog box. Then double-click any of the handles around the label to resize it.

Changing a label's caption

4. Repeat step 3 to change the Caption properties of the two unbound labels to read *# of Days Late* and *Fines Due*. Then adjust their size and position to look like the one shown on the next page.

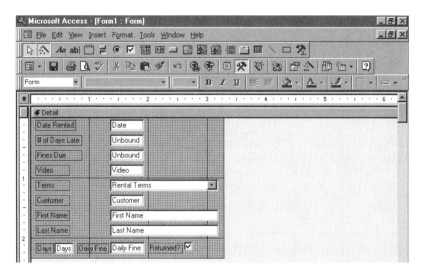

5. Click the first Unbound control, click the Properties button, change its Name property to *Days Late*, and change its Text Align property to Right (you'll have to scroll the properties list).

6. Repeat step 5 for the second Unbound control, changing its Name property to *Fines*.

   Back in the form, Unbound has not changed, but the names in the Object box at the left end of the Formatting toolbar are now Days Late and Fines, respectively.

   Now let's use the Unbound controls to build formulas to calculate the number of days late and the fine. Follow these steps:

Specifying the source of a control's value

1. Double-click the first Unbound control to display the Properties dialog box, click anywhere in the Control Source property edit box, and then click the Build button to display the Expression Builder dialog box shown here:

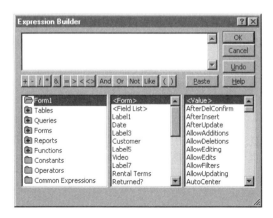

The open Form1 folder represents the unnamed form you are creating, and all its controls and labels are listed in the middle box. You need to use these elements to build a formula that calculates how late the video is. That formula is then the source of the control's value.

The video's due date is the day it was rented plus the number of days it was rented for. For example, if a video was rented on 7/15/97 for two days, it would be due back at Brock Buster's Video on 7/15/97+2, or 7/17/97. Let's start with this calculation:

2. Double-click the Date field in the middle box and type +. Then scroll the middle box and double-click the Days field (the formula is now *[Date]+[Days]*).

The number of days the video is overdue is the difference between the due date and today's date. Ordinarily, you would use the Date() function for today's date, but because you are using fabricated dates for the sample database, let's pretend that today's date is 7/28/97:

3. Change the formula in the Expression Builder dialog box so that it reads as follows:

=#7/28/97#-([Date]+[Days])

4. Click OK and close the Properties dialog box. Access displays the formula in the control.

5. Now repeat step 1 for the second Unbound control. In the Expression Builder dialog box, double-click Daily Fine in the middle box, type *, double-click Days Late (the formula is now *[Daily Fine]*[Days Late]*), and click OK.

6. In the Properties dialog box, change the Format property to Currency, and close the dialog box. The form now looks like the one shown on the next page. (We've enlarged the two calculated controls so that you can see the formulas, but you should make these controls the same size as the Date control above them.)

Bound vs. unbound controls

A bound control is linked to a field in a table. You use bound controls to display and enter field values. An unbound control isn't linked to another database element unless you establish the link. You can use unbound controls to display information that is not in your tables, such as instructions to the user, or you can establish a link to an existing database element by clicking the arrow button in the Control Source edit box of the Properties dialog box and selecting the element from the drop-down list.

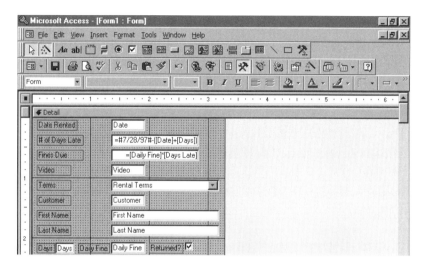

Total row calculation options

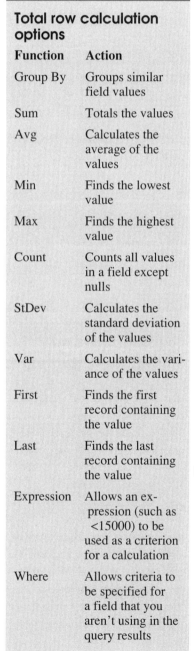

Function	Action
Group By	Groups similar field values
Sum	Totals the values
Avg	Calculates the average of the values
Min	Finds the lowest value
Max	Finds the highest value
Count	Counts all values in a field except nulls
StDev	Calculates the standard deviation of the values
Var	Calculates the variance of the values
First	Finds the first record containing the value
Last	Finds the last record containing the value
Expression	Allows an expression (such as <15000) to be used as a criterion for a calculation
Where	Allows criteria to be specified for a field that you aren't using in the query results

7. Click the Save button and save the form as *Late Videos.* Then switch to form view to see your masterpiece. Here's what the form looks like after we adjusted the size of the controls to correspond better to their contents:

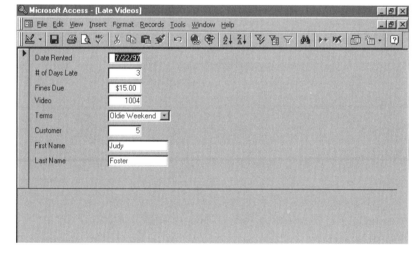

8. Close the form.

Using the Total Row in Queries

Access provides a quick and easy way to perform calculations on field values in a query. Using the Total row in the QBE grid, we can find the average, sum, highest value, lowest value, and even the standard deviation and the variance of the values.

Let's say, for example, that Mr. Buster wants to know how many videos were rented on any given day. He doesn't want to know which videos or any other information, just the count of videos rented. Follow these steps to get Mr. Buster what he needs:

1. First add some rental transactions to the Rentals table, simulating several rentals on each of the dates already in the table. (Assign the Terms values randomly, but be sure to click the Returned? check box for the earlier dates.)

2. Create a new query based on the Rentals table and move the Date and Video fields to the QBE grid.

3. Click the Totals button on the toolbar. Access displays a Total row below the Table row, like this:

The Totals button

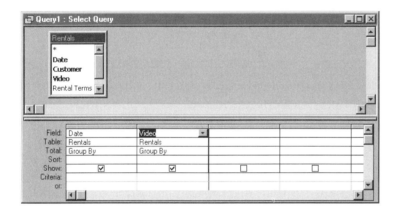

4. Click the Total row in the Video column and then click the arrow button to display a drop-down list of calculation options.

5. From the drop-down list, select Count. The word *Count* replaces *Group By* in the Total row. (The Group By option tells Access to group similar values in that particular field; see the tip on the facing page for definitions of other options.)

The Count function

6. Click the Save button and save the query as *Daily Count*.

7. Run the query. The results for the rental transactions that we entered in the Rentals table in step 1 are shown on the next page (your results will be different, depending on the transactions you entered).

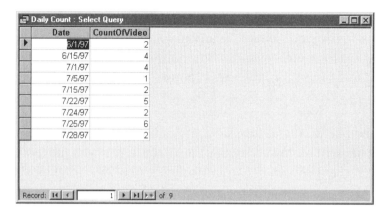

The Count function changes the name of the Video field to CountOfVideo and displays the number of videos that were rented on each day.

8. Close the query, and if necessary, close the Rentals table.

Using Graphs in Forms

The information in the previous example is useful, but visually bland. Often information can be presented more dramatically using a graph, so let's create a form that displays a graph of the number of videos rented each day. Follow these steps:

1. Click the Forms tab in the database window and create a new blank form in design view.

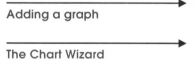

Adding a graph

The Chart Wizard

2. Choose Chart from the Insert menu and draw a rectangle on the form. When you release the mouse button, the first Chart Wizard dialog box appears. (If a message box tells you to install the Chart Wizard, see the adjacent tip.)

Installing the Chart Wizard

The Chart Wizard is not part of the typical Access installation. Like the Input Mask Wizard, the Chart Wizard is included in the Advanced Wizards component of the program. To install the Chart Wizard, rerun the Setup program, click Add/Remove, and select the Access Advanced Wizard option.

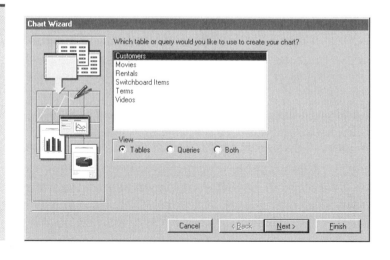

3. Click Queries in the View section, and with Daily Count selected in the list, click Next to display this dialog box:

Specifying the base

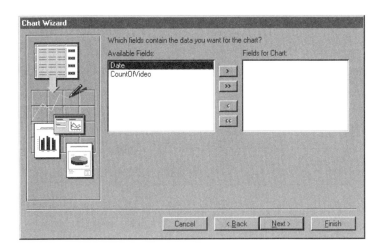

4. Move both the Date and CountOfVideo fields to the Fields For Chart box and then click Next to display these graph options:

Specifying the fields

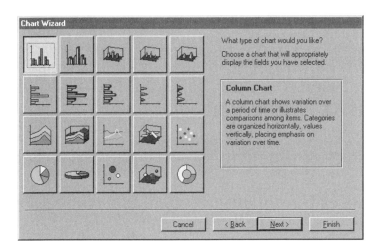

5. Check each graph type in turn and read its description so that you know what's available. Then select the first option in the first row—the 2-D column chart—and click Next to display the dialog box shown on the next page.

Specifying the graph type

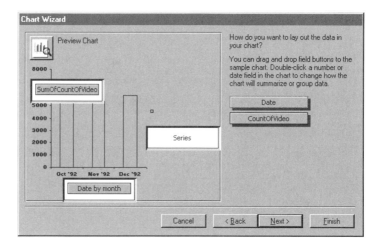

Here, you can preview the graph and go back and change its type if necessary. You can also change the grouping of the fields represented on each axis.

Changing the grouping

6. Double-click the Date By Month control on the preview's x-axis, select Day in the Group dialog box that appears, and click OK. Then click Finish to close the Chart Wizard.

Back on the form, Access displays a placeholder graph to designate the area the graph will fill.

7. Save the form as *Daily Count* and switch to form view to see the real graph in place, like this:

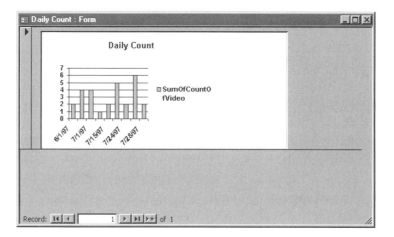

How your graph looks depends on the size of the rectangle you drew in step 2.

Graphs often need to be edited significantly before they look the way we want them to. This editing is accomplished in a separate editing environment created by a program called Microsoft Graph. Let's use this program to edit the graph on the form:

Microsoft Graph

1. Switch to design view, right-click the graph, and choose Chart Object and then Edit from the object menu. Microsoft Graph opens with a placeholder graph displayed in a window and its datasheet in the background, like this:

Editing graphs

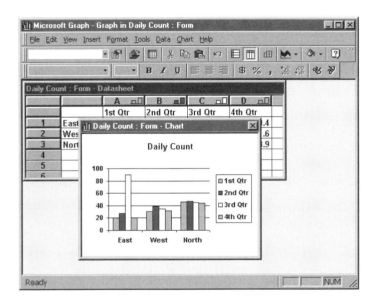

2. Choose Chart Options from the Chart menu and then click the Gridlines tab to display this dialog box:

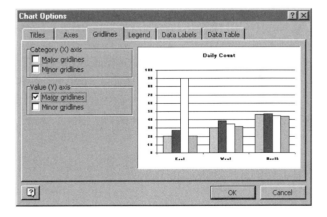

Microsoft Graph

Microsoft Graph is the graphing program that ships with Access. You can use Microsoft Graph as a stand-alone program, but you will generally use it in conjunction with Access (or with the other Microsoft Office programs). The Graph program has its own help system, so if you are interested in exploring its capabilities further, check out the topics available on its Help menu.

3. In the Value (Y) axis section, click the Major Gridlines check box to deselect it, and then click OK to remove the gridlines.

4. Click any of the graph's blue columns (these columns plot the first series of data—in our case, the only series of data). Handles appear on all the columns to indicate that they are selected.

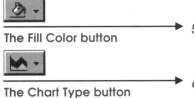

The Fill Color button

The Chart Type button

5. Click the arrow to the right of the Fill Color button and select yellow from the drop-down palette.

6. Click the arrow to the right of the Chart Type button, and select the different types in turn. (If you select a format that is incompatible with the data, Graph displays a message box.) Finish by reselecting the 2-D column type (the first option in the third row).

7. Because this graph is very simple, you don't really need the legend. Click it once to select it and then press the Delete key.

Deleting the legend

8. Since we know there are several dates to display along the y-axis of the graph, widen the chart window until it almost fills the Graph window.

Types of graphs

Listed below are the main types of graphs you can create in Access. The type of graph you select should take into account the kind of data you want to display.

- **Bar graphs** are ideal for displaying the values of several items at a single point in time.
- **Column graphs** are the best choice for displaying the variations in the value of a single item over time.
- **Line graphs** are often used to show variations in the values of more than one item over time.
- **Area graphs** are similar to line graphs except that they plot multiple data series as cumulative layers with different colors, patterns, or shades.
- **Pie graphs** are good for displaying the percentages of an item that can be assigned to the item's components.
- **Scatter graphs** are great for plotting two values to see if there is any correlation between them.
- **Combination graphs** can show two different types of graphs at once; for example, combinations of line and bar graphs, or bar and area graphs.
- **3-D graphs** are useful for displaying data with two or more variables. 3-D formats are available for these types of graphs: line, bar, column, area, and pie.

Other available types of graphs include the doughnut, radar, bubble, surface, stock, core, cylinder, and pyramid. For more information, see Graph's online help.

9. Click the Close button to close Microsoft Graph and return to design view.

10. Switch to form view to check the display of the graph and then, if necessary, switch back to design view and widen the graph's frame by dragging the middle handle to the right until you can see the entire graph. When you switch back to form view, the graph looks like this:

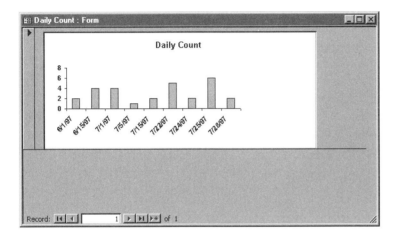

11. Close the form, saving your changes.

A full tour of Microsoft Graph is beyond the scope of this book. If you are familiar with other Microsoft applications, most of the options are fairly intuitive, and you can always turn to Graph's Help menu if you get stuck.

Well, you made it through our examples of some of the more advanced uses of forms and queries. Use these examples as springboards for your own ideas, and you'll soon discover an infinite variety of ways to retrieve and display information.

Maintaining and Managing a Database

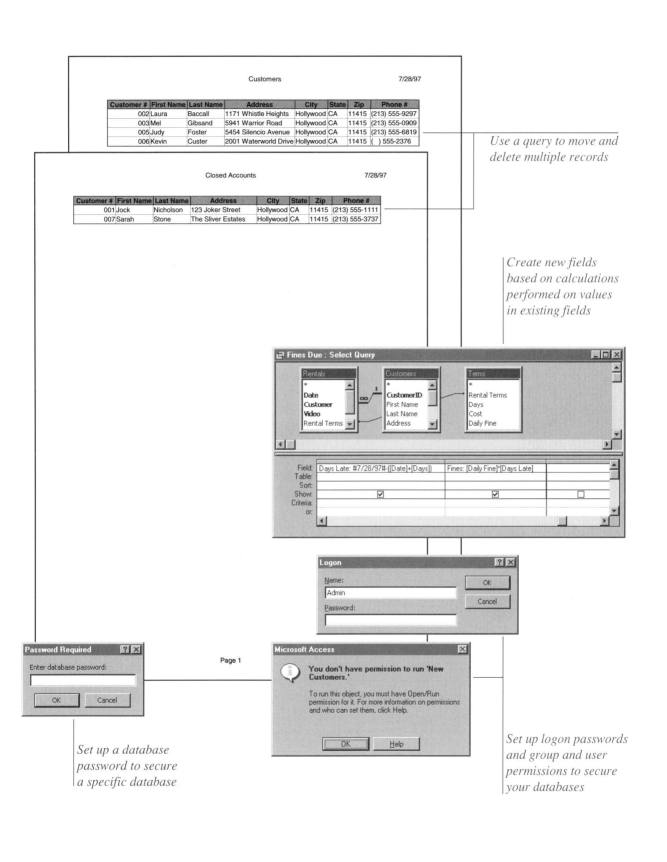

Customers   7/28/97

Customer #	First Name	Last Name	Address	City	State	Zip	Phone #
002	Laura	Baccall	1171 Whistle Heights	Hollywood	CA	11415	(213) 555-9297
003	Mel	Gibsand	5941 Warrior Road	Hollywood	CA	11415	(213) 555-0909
005	Judy	Foster	5454 Silencio Avenue	Hollywood	CA	11415	(213) 555-6819
006	Kevin	Custer	2001 Waterworld Drive	Hollywood	CA	11415	( ) 555-2376

Use a query to move and delete multiple records

Closed Accounts   7/28/97

Customer #	First Name	Last Name	Address	City	State	Zip	Phone #
001	Jock	Nicholson	123 Joker Street	Hollywood	CA	11415	(213) 555-1111
007	Sarah	Stone	The Sliver Estates	Hollywood	CA	11415	(213) 555-3737

Create new fields based on calculations performed on values in existing fields

Fines Due : Select Query

Rentals
*
Date
Customer
Video
Rental Terms

Customers
*
CustomerID
First Name
Last Name
Address

Terms
*
Rental Terms
Days
Cost
Daily Fine

Field:	Days Late: #7/28/97#-([Date]+[Days])	Fines: [Daily Fine]*[Days Late]	
Table:			
Sort:			
Show:	☑	☑	☐
Criteria:			
or:			

Logon

Name:
Admin

Password:

OK

Cancel

Password Required

Enter database password:

OK   Cancel

Page 1

Microsoft Access

You don't have permission to run 'New Customers.'

To run this object, you must have Open/Run permission for it. For more information on permissions and who can set them, click Help.

OK   Help

Set up a database password to secure a specific database

Set up logon passwords and group and user permissions to secure your databases

In this chapter, we discuss issues relating to ongoing maintenance of databases and managing them from a security point of view. We start by showing you how to maintain a switchboard, modifying it so that it always reflects the changing contents of its database. Then we look at ways to keep databases up-to-date and how to build in the flexibility to meet future needs. Up until now, we have dealt with only one record at a time and one user at a time. In the real world, however, we generally work with several records and several users. You'll get a feeling for how to manipulate multiple records in the first part of the chapter, and we'll talk about how to handle multiple users in the second part.

More About Switchboards

Since creating the switchboard in Chapter 3, we have added several forms, queries, and reports to the Brock Buster's Video database. We could add all of these objects to the main switchboard, but it would then be cluttered and possibly confusing for new users. To avoid this problem, we can link a series of switchboards to the main switchboard to lead new users through various options, much like the folders and subfolders used in the Windows 95 environment.

As a demonstration, let's construct a switchboard containing all the reports in the database and link it to the main switchboard. Follow these steps to create a new switchboard:

Modifying a switchboard

When modifying a switchboard created by the Database Wizard, you should always use the Switchboard Manager rather than trying to make the modifications in design view. A switchboard form works by using entries in the Switchboard Items table that describe what the buttons on the form display and do. So, if you try to make design changes to the switchboard form, the application may stop working.

1. With the Brock Buster's Video database window open on your screen, choose Add-Ins and then Switchboard Manager from the Tools menu.

2. In the Switchboard Manager dialog box, click New, and name the new switchboard *Reports Switchboard*. Click OK.

3. Select Reports Switchboard and click Edit.

4. To add an item to this switchboard, click New in the Edit Switchboard Page dialog box. Type *Customer Mailing Labels* in the Text edit box, change the Command setting to Open Report, and change the Report setting to Customer Mailing Labels. Then click OK.

5. Repeat step 4 to create a switchboard item called *Movies By Rating* that opens the Movies report.

6. Close the Edit Switchboard Page dialog box.

Now we've created a switchboard, but we have yet to link it to our main switchboard. Here are the steps:

1. Select Main Switchboard, click Edit, and then click New in the Edit Switchboard Page dialog box.

   Linking switchboards

2. In the Edit Switchboard Page dialog box, type *Print reports* in the Text edit box, leave Go To Switchboard as the Command setting, and then select Reports Switchboard as the Switchboard setting. Click OK.

3. Click Close twice to close the Edit Switchboard Page dialog box and then the Switchboard Manager dialog box.

Now test the new switchboard:

1. Move to the Forms tab in the database window, select Switchboard, and click Open. Access opens the Main Switchboard (see page 84), where a new Print Reports item is listed.

   Testing the links

2. Click the Print Reports check box. Access jumps to the new switchboard, where the reports are listed as shown here:

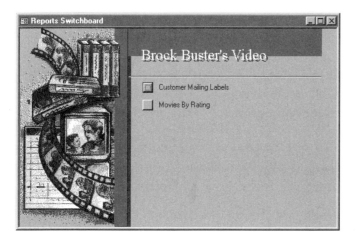

3. Click one of the reports to jump directly to its window. Then close that window and click the other report to test its link.

4. Close the report window and then close the switchboard.

Working with More than One Record

Maintaining a database would be an arduous task if we were limited to working with single records. Fortunately, Access provides several ways to perform actions on multiple records.

Creating New Tables with Queries

Sometimes we will want to create a new table using some of the records in an existing table. We could reenter all the records in a new table; or we could save the existing table with a new name and then delete the records we don't want. A third possibility is to use a query to extract the records we want into a datasheet that we then turn into the new table.

Let's look at an example. In Chapter 5, we used a form to calculate the fines due on late videos. Suppose we now realize we need that information in table format to be able to generate reports. Let's create a Fines Due query and then convert the query datasheet to a table. Here are the steps:

1. On the Queries tab of the database window, select the Late Videos query and open it in design view.

2. Choose Save As/Export from the File menu and save the query with the name *Fines Due*.

3. Select and delete the First Name and Last Name columns.

4. Click the Show boxes of the Video, Rental Terms, Returned?, Days, and Daily Fine fields to tell Access not to display these fields in the query datasheet.

Calculations in queries →

5. In the Field row of the next blank column, type the following formula, which is the same as the one used to calculate the number of days late in the Late Videos form (see page 129):

#7/28/97#-([Date]+[Days])

6. Click the Show box in this column twice to tell Access to include the results of the formula in the query datasheet.

7. Notice that Access has entered *Expr1* in front of the formula as the name of the field that will hold the formula results. Replace this name with *Days Late* (leave the colon).

Naming the calculated field

8. Repeat steps 5 through 7 to enter the following formula in the next available column:

   Fines: [Daily Fine]*[Days Late]

9. Double-click the right border of the thin gray box above the Field row of the Days Late field to widen the column to fit its contents. Repeat this step for the Fines field. Here's what the formulas look like:

Widening QBE grid columns

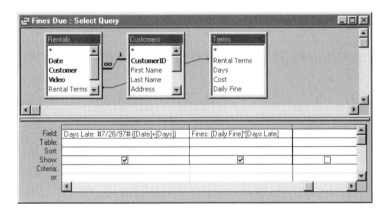

Now tell Access to turn the results of the query into a new table. We do this by changing the type of the query, like this:

1. Click the arrow to the right of the Query Type button on the toolbar and select Make Table Query from the drop-down list. Access displays this dialog box:

The Query Type button

2. Type *Overdue* in the Table Name edit box and press Enter. (The new table's name can't be the same as the query name.)

3. Now run the query. Access displays the dialog box shown on the next page. (Your number of rows may be different.)

4. Click Yes to create the table, click the Save button to save the query, and then close the query window. In the database window, Access identifies the make table query with a distinctive icon.

For peace of mind, let's verify that Access successfully created the table:

1. Click the Tables tab, select the Overdue table, and open it in datasheet view.

2. To display the Fines field values as dollars, click the View button to switch to design view, click anywhere in the Fines field, set its Format property to Currency, and save your changes. Then click the View button again to see the results, which reflect the rentals you entered in Chapter 5:

Date	Customer	Days Late	Fines
7/22/97	5	3	$15.00
7/24/97	5	3	$15.00
7/25/97	2	2	$20.00
7/24/97	5	3	$30.00
7/22/97	1	3	$15.00
7/22/97	1	5	$50.00
7/22/97	1	5	$50.00
7/22/97	3	5	$50.00
7/25/97	2	2	$20.00
7/25/97	2	2	$20.00
7/25/97	2	2	$20.00
7/25/97	1	2	$20.00
7/25/97	1	2	$20.00

Record: 1 of 13

3. Close the table.

Updating Records with Queries

From time to time, we may want to change a value in several records in a table. For example, if we assign a new salesperson

Caution: rerunning make table queries

Make table queries can be very useful, but be aware of the difference between make table and append queries. If you run a make table query and the table already exists, the query will overwrite the existing table, whereas an append query will add its results to an existing table.

to a sales area, we may need to change the salesperson's name in records in a Customers or Invoices table.

For demonstration purposes, suppose Hollywood is assigned a new Zip code, and we need to update the Customers table to reflect the change. We could update each record in turn, but an easier way is to use an update query. Follow these steps:

1. With Customers selected on the Tables tab of the database window, choose Query from the New Object button's drop-down list and click OK to open a new query based on the Customers table in design view.

2. Double-click the PostalCode field to add it to the QBE grid.

3. Choose Update Query from the Query Type button's drop-down list. Access changes the select query to an update query and adds an Update To row to the QBE grid.

Specifying an update query

4. In the Update To row of the PostalCode column, type *11415*.

The Update To row

5. In the Criteria row, type *11403*, and press Enter. The query looks like this:

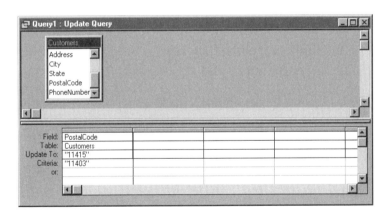

6. Run the query. Access advises you of the number of records to be updated in this dialog box:

Caution: leaving the Criteria row blank

In an update query, if you enter information in the Update To row but leave the Criteria row blank, Access assumes you want to make the change no matter what the existing field value is. The result is that Access updates every record in the table. So be careful when you run update queries!

7. Click Yes to complete the changes and then close the query without saving it.

8. Open the Customers table, where all the records for customers who live in Hollywood now have the new Zip code.

For a small table, it may be much faster to make the changes manually. For large tables, using an update query is definitely faster and ensures that all the affected records are changed.

Moving Records with Queries

There are a few things we have not considered in the Brock Buster's Video database. One is what to do when a customer closes an account. If we keep all the customer records, both active and inactive, in the Customers table, the table may soon become too large to work with on a daily basis. Also, we may want to keep additional information about closed customer accounts, such as whether they owe any fines.

One solution is to create a separate Closed Accounts table in the database and to move inactive customers from the Customers table to the Closed Accounts table. To work through this example, we need to add a Closed field to the Customers table:

1. Open the Customers table in design view, add a Closed field below PhoneNumber, set the data type to Yes/No, type *No* as the Default Value property, and save your changes.

2. Switch to datasheet view, change the Closed values for Jock Nicholson and Sarah Stone to Yes, and close the table.

Now we're ready to create the Closed Accounts table:

1. With Customers selected in the database window, click the Copy button on the toolbar and then click the Paste button. Access displays this dialog box:

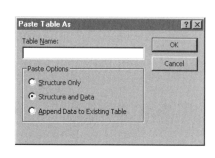

2. In the Table Name edit box, type *Closed Accounts*, click the Structure Only option, and click OK. Access adds the new table to the list in the database window.

3. Open the Closed Accounts table in design view and delete the Closed field by clicking its row selector and pressing Delete. (All the records in this table are for closed accounts so this field is redundant.)

4. Create a new Amount Due field, set the data type to Number, and the Format property to Currency.

5. Close the table, saving your changes when prompted.

   We can now move the closed records from the Customers table to the Closed Accounts table. This is a two-step, append-and-delete operation, as you'll see if you follow the steps in the next two sections.

Appending Records

We now have a table in which to store the records for the customers that are inactive. Follow these steps to move these records to the Closed Accounts table:

1. Select the Customers table on the Tables tab of the database window, select Query from the New Object button's drop-down list, and click OK to open the query in design view.

2. Add all the fields from the Customers box to the QBE grid by double-clicking the Customers title bar, pointing to the selected fields, and dragging the pointer to the QBE grid.

3. Type *Yes* in the Criteria row of the Closed column.

4. Now select Append Query from the Query Type button's drop-down list. Access displays this dialog box:

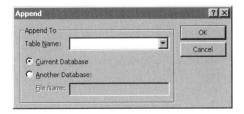

Specifying an append query

5. Click the arrow to the right of the Table Name edit box, select *Closed Accounts* as the name of the table to which you want to append the results of the query, and click OK.

6. Run the query. Access advises you that it will append two rows, like this:

7. Click Yes to proceed with the query and then close it, saving it as *Append Closed Accounts*.

8. Now open the Closed Accounts table to verify that it contains the two closed records, as shown here:

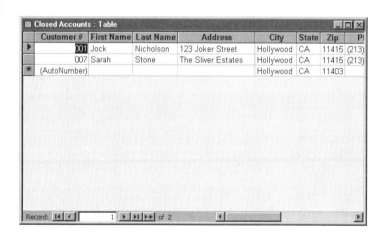

9. Close the table.

Because we saved the query, we can run it whenever we need to append records from the Customers table to the Closed Accounts table.

Deleting Records

We have copied the closed records to the Closed Accounts table, but the records still exist in the Customers table. We

---

Crosstab queries

Crosstab queries are a useful way of displaying data in a grid format—similar to a pivot table in spreadsheets—so that the data is easier to compare. For example, a crosstab query could be used to compare the number of rentals for each customer, grouped by rental type. To set up a crosstab query, you can select the Crosstab Query Wizard from the New Query dialog box or you can create a new query for the appropriate tables, add the fields you want to the QBE grid, and then select Crosstab Query from the Query Type drop-down list to add a Crosstab row and a Total row to the QBE grid. Use the options in the Crosstab row to determine which fields are rows, columns, and values. Then set up the functions you need in the Total row and run the query. The datasheet is displayed as a grid with the row and column headings you specified in the Crosstab row.

could easily delete them individually because there are only two. But what if we want to delete many records that are scattered throughout the table? A better technique is to set up a query to delete the records for us. Follow these steps:

1. Create a new query based on the Customers table and open it in design view.

2. Add all the fields in the Customers box to the QBE grid.

3. Select Delete Query from the Query Type button's drop-down list. Access adds a Delete row to the QBE grid with Where in each column.

◄——— Specifying a delete query

4. In the Criteria row of the Closed column, type *Yes* to tell Access to delete all the records where the closed field value is Yes.

5. Save the query as *Delete Closed Accounts*.

6. Without changing any of the entries in the grid, run the query. When Access advises you that two records will be deleted, click Yes to proceed. Access then displays this message:

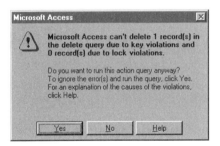

The results demonstrate how Access safeguards our databases by preventing us from introducing errors. Access does not tell us exactly what the problem is, but it does tell us that deleting one of the records will produce *key violations*, meaning that the record is referenced by at least one record in a related table. Even if we click Yes in this dialog box, the offending record will not be deleted. Turn the page, and we'll see where the problem lies.

Pivot tables

If you are familiar with Excel and would like to display your data in a pivot table, an alternative to creating a crosstab query is to create a form by selecting Pivot-Table Wizard in the New Form dialog box. Access then walks you through the steps of creating a pivot table. Clicking a button on the newly created pivot-table form opens Excel so that you can edit the pivot table directly. (The underlying data is not affected).

1. Click No, and then click the Database Window button (shown on page 64) on the toolbar.

Tracking relationships

2. With Customers selected in the list of tables, click the Relationships button on the toolbar to display the relationships you've established between the tables of the Brock Buster's Video database, as shown here:

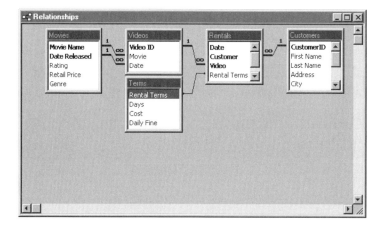

The Customers table has only one relationship linking CustomerID to Customer in the Rentals table. So this must be the relationship that is causing the key violation.

Displaying relationship properties

3. Click the thin part of the line between Customer ID and Customer to select the line, right-click, and choose Edit Relationship from the object menu to display this dialog box:

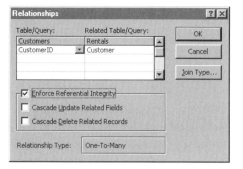

As you can see, the relationship between CustomerID and Customer is One-To-Many with referential integrity enforced.

Because of the referential integrity, you have a tough decision to make:

- If you turn off the Enforce Referential Integrity option, Access will allow you to enter Customer values in the Rentals table that do not correspond to CustomerID values in the Customers table. For example, a clerk would be able to rent a movie to customer 3000 when no such customer exists.

- If you want to leave referential integrity in force, you could remove all records from the Rentals table involving the customer whose records you are trying to delete only from the Customers table. (You might want to create a Closed Accounts Rental History table and store these records there. However, compiling rental information would then be more difficult. If Mrs. Buster wanted to know how many videos were rented in a given month, you would need to remember to include these closed rental transactions in the calculation.)

There is no easy answer to this problem. The solution depends on which is more important to the Busters: complete rental information in one table or a built-in check on the Customer values entered by the clerks. For this example, let's turn off the Enforce Referential Integrity option and assume that the Busters train their clerks well:

4. Deselect the Enforce Referential Integrity option in the Relationships dialog box, click OK, and then close the Relationships window.

5. Click the title bar of the Delete Closed Accounts window to activate the query and then rerun the query, clicking Yes to delete the two closed records.

6. Close the query.

Databases are rarely static. As you have seen, we can use queries to efficiently maintain a database by dealing with multiple records or entire tables at once.

Database replication

If you need to create copies of a database for use at multiple sites (for example, branch offices), you can use database replication to ensure that although each site works on its own copy, any changes can all be incorporated back into the original version. Database replication is beyond the scope of this book. If you need to use this feature, consult the online help system, or check out this topic in *Building Applications with Microsoft Access 97*, which ships with Access. (If you have the professional version of Office 97, this book is available as part of the ValuPack on the CD-ROM.)

Dealing with More than One User

Databases created for small businesses and the home often have only one user. However, in large businesses, one or two people usually create and maintain the database, but many other people use the database to update and retrieve information. Brock Buster's Video, for example, may have several clerks who use the database but are not allowed to change its design or structure. Because a database is only as good as the integrity of its information, securing the database is often critical, but it can also be a headache.

Setting a Password for a Database

The simplest method of securing a database that won't be replicated is to assign a password for opening it. This method is most useful when only a few people use the database and each is trustworthy and knowledgable enough to have full access to all database components. Follow these steps to assign a password:

1. Close the Brock Buster's Video database. If you are asked whether you want to empty the Clipboard, click Yes.

Temporarily locking out other users

2. Click the Open Database button on the toolbar to display the Open dialog box, and with Brock Buster's Video selected, click the Exclusive option just below the Advanced button and then click Open.

3. Choose Security and then Set Database Password from the Tools menu to display this dialog box:

The Exclusive option

When you open a database with the Exclusive option selected, you shut out any other users of the database while you have it open. This option is very useful on networked computers, but not as important to single computer users.

4. In both the Password and Verify edit boxes, type *opensesame* and click OK. (Passwords are case sensitive, so keep it all lowercase.)

5. Close the database and then try to reopen it. Access displays this dialog box:

6. Type *opensesame* in the edit box and press Enter.

Setting Security for Several Users

Security in Access is a complicated affair, based on a system of *groups* to which password-protected *user accounts* are assigned. By default, two groups are created by Access: *Admins* and *Users*. Admins is an elite group, reserved for database administrators with omnipotent powers; Users is not so picky. In fact, all accounts are automatically assigned to Users as well as to more specific groups. By default, one user account is set up with the name *Admin* and is assigned to both the Admins and Users groups. When we start Access, the program assumes that we are this Admin user, logs us on without requiring a password, and gives us unrestricted power over any database we create or open, unless that database has been secured.

The default groups

The default user

Securing a database involves several steps, and any missteps can produce unexpected results. We'll walk you through the process (and then walk you back) but here's a brief overview of what you need to do:

- Use the Workgroup Administrator to create a new workgroup information file, which identifies groups and their members.

- Add a new user to the Admins group.

- Remove the Admin user from Admins so that Admin is a member of the Users group only, and then assign a password to the Admin user.

- Restart Access as the new user.

- Create a new database and remove all Users group permissions for each object type in that database.

Deleting database passwords

You can delete a database password—for example, the *opensesame* password we created for the Brock Buster's Video database. First open the database by displaying the Open dialog box, selecting the database you want to open, clicking the Exclusive option, and clicking Open. Then enter the password. Next, choose Security and then Unset Database Password from the Tools menu. Type the current password in the Password edit box and then click OK. You now will no longer need to enter a password to open the database.

- Import the objects from the original database into the new database.

- Create groups and users as necessary and assign group and user permissions that control what a user can do.

Seem like a lot of work? It is, but the result—a controlled database environment—is worth it if our data is critical to our company's operations. In the next section, we'll explain the steps in more detail.

Caution!

A Note of Caution: The workgroup information file, groups, and user accounts operate at the program level, not at the database level. Users identify themselves when the program starts, not when a database opens. Unless you have complete control of Access on your system, be sure to consult with other program users before you begin changing this level of security.

Creating a Secure Workgroup

The workgroup
information file

Access stores all information about groups, users, and passwords in a separate file that is stored in the main Access folder. When the program was installed, Access, by default, associated the user name and the company name with this file. As you can imagine, this combination would be fairly easy to discover if you were attempting to break into a database. So Access won't let us change any of the program's security information until we customize this file and give it a password. Follow these steps to make this change:

1. Close Access. Open Windows Explorer, navigate to the Program Files/Microsoft Office folder, and find the MS Access Workgroup Administrator shortcut.

The Workgroup Administrator
program

2. Double-click the shortcut to start the Workgroup Administrator program, as shown here:

3. Click Create to display this dialog box:

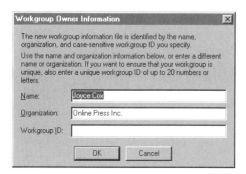

4. Type your name and organization. In the Workgroup ID edit box, type a password you will easily recall. It can be any combination of up to 20 letters and numbers, and it is case sensitive. **Important:** Before you click OK, be sure to write down all the information from this dialog box. If you ever need to recreate this file, there is no way to retrieve this information from your computer.

Important!

5. Click OK to display this dialog box:

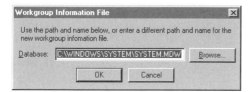

6. Change the name of the file to something memorable and click OK. (We chose NEWSYS.MDW. You can leave the file as SYSTEM.MDW if you want.) Access then displays this confirmation:

Splitting a database

Another useful tool for managing a database accessed by multiple users on a network is the Database Splitter. This tool separates a database so that its tables are stored in one file and its forms, queries, and reports are stored in another. Users on the network can then create their own forms, queries, and reports to extract information from the database's tables, but they can't change them: the tables remain intact in their own file. To split a database, choose Add-Ins and then Database Splitter from the Tools menu and follow the instructions presented by the Database Splitter Wizard.

7. If everything looks correct, click OK. Then click OK to close the confirmation message box, and click Exit to quit the Workgroup Administrator program. Finally, close Windows Explorer.

Behind the scenes, Access records in the Windows Registry the name of the workgroup information file to be used whenever we start Access.

Creating User Accounts

Now that we have taken this first security measure, Access will allow us to create new groups and users. Let's start by creating an Owner account in the existing Admins group. Follow these steps:

1. Start Access and open the Brock Buster's Video database, entering the *opensesame* password when prompted.

2. From the Tools menu, choose Security and then User And Group Accounts. Access displays this dialog box:

3. Click New in the User section to display this dialog box:

4. Type *Owner* in both the Name edit box and the Personal ID edit box and click OK.

Names, personal IDs, and passwords

The personal ID (PID) you enter in the New User/Group dialog box is combined with the name you enter to create an encrypted security ID (SID), which Access stores in the workgroup information file and uses to identify each account. You need to accurately record each account's name and PID so that you can recreate the account if the workgroup information file becomes damaged. After you create an account you assign it a password. This password is exactly what you would expect it to be: a unique identifier associated with the user's name for purposes of logging on to Access.

By default, the Owner account is listed only as a member of the all-purpose Users group, which you will usually want to have the most restricted access to databases. You want the Owner account to have unlimited access, so you need to add it to the Admins group, which by default is unrestricted.

5. With Admins selected in the Available Groups section, click the Add button. Admins is added to the list that defines which groups the Owner account is a member of.

Adding users to groups

6. You want Owner to be the only account with unlimited access to databases, so select Admin from the Name drop-down list in the User section, and remove it from the Admins group by clicking Remove with the Admins group selected in the Member Of list.

Removing users from groups

7. Currently, the Admin account has no password. To create a password, click the Change Logon Password tab and type *Brock* in the New Password and Verify edit boxes. Then click OK to close the User And Group Accounts dialog box.

Changing passwords

8. Close Access completely, saving any changes if prompted.

The advantage of activating security at the program level is that users enter their passwords only once, and Access passes their security information to any databases they open.

Creating a Secure Database

The current Brock Buster's Video database is "owned" by its creator, the default Admin user. We need to create a secure version of this database that can be modified only by the Owner user. (From now on, we will only be using the secure version of the database so that we can return to the original Brock Buster's Video database if we make any mistakes.) Follow these steps:

1. Restart Access. This message box appears:

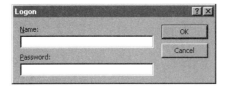

Good and bad passwords

Passwords that are easy to decipher can give users a false sense of security. Birth dates and social security numbers are obvious examples of bad passwords. Using common words is also inappropriate, however, because some "hackers" use computer programs that run through entire dictionaries, trying each word until they find the password. A good rule for passwords is to use letters and symbols to form nonsensical words, always longer than four characters. Try substituting + for N, $ for S, or @ for A to form passwords such as *$uperm@+*, *$ale$*, and *ope+$e$ame*.

2. Type *Owner* in the Name edit box, leave the Password edit box blank, and then click OK. (For convenience, we don't assign passwords to the accounts we create in our examples. However, in practice, you probably would want to password-protect all accounts.)

3. Create a blank database called *Secure Brock Buster's Video*.

Permissions →

Having created the database, you need to specify who can do what with it. The right to perform a particular activity is called a *permission*, and you can grant permissions to individual users or to an entire group of users. A user always has the permissions assigned to his or her group; you can't take any away. But you can give a user more permissions than those assigned to his or her group. This setup is flexible yet efficient, because you can usually make changes in one place—at the group level—instead of having to work with several different user accounts. Here's a list of the available permissions:

This permission...	Allows users to...
Open/Run	Open databases, forms, and reports and run macros
Open Exclusive	Open databases, locking out other users
Read Data	View data in tables and queries
Update Data	View and modify data but not insert or delete data in tables and queries
Insert Data	View and insert data but not modify or delete it in tables and queries
Delete Data	View and delete data but not modify or insert it in tables and queries
Read Design	View tables, queries, forms, reports, macros, and modules in design view
Modify Design	View, change the design of, and delete tables, queries, forms, reports, macros, and modules
Administer	Set passwords, replicate, and change startup properties of databases; work with objects and data in tables, queries, forms, reports, macros, and modules in any way; assign permissions to others

Let's remove the default permissions of the Users group:

1. Choose Security and then User And Group Permissions from the Tools menu to display this dialog box:

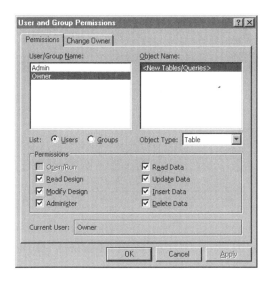

For each object in a database, you can assign any of the applicable permissions to a user or group. A check mark signifies that the permission has been granted.

2. Click the Groups option button and select Users in the User/- Group Name list box. As you can see, this group starts with unlimited access, so you must tell Access what members of this group *can't* do, rather than what they can do, by unchecking boxes.

3. With Table selected in the Object Type box and <New Tables/Queries> selected in the Object Name list, deselect all the check boxes in the Permissions section, and click Apply.

4. Change the Object Type to Form, deselect all the permissions, and click Apply.

5. Repeat step 4 for all the database components in the Object Type drop-down list except Database (at the top of the list). Then click OK.

Now let's import the components of the unsecure Brock Buster's Video database into the new secure database. Follow the steps on the next page.

Removing the Users group permissions

Who has what permissions?

If you check a particular user's permissions in the User And Group Permissions dialog box, it may appear that the user has no permissions when in fact he or she has all the permissions assigned to his or her group. Always check the group's permissions first, because the user can have more permissions than the group but not fewer permissions.

Importing database
components

1. Choose Get External Data and then Import from the File menu to display the Import dialog box. Select Brock Buster's Video and click Import. Type the *opensesame* password when prompted and click OK. This dialog box appears:

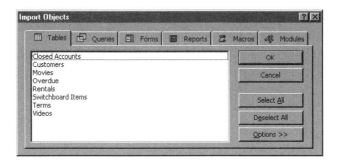

2. Click Select All on the Tables tab, then click the Queries tab, and click Select All again. Repeat this step to select all the objects on all the tabs, and then click OK.

   We now have a secure version of the Brock Buster's Video database that can be accessed only by the Owner user.

Creating Groups

The next step is to create groups for the users we want to be able to work with the database. Only members of the Admins group can create groups. For this example, let's create a group called *Clerks* that is not as restricted as the Users group:

1. Choose Security and then User And Group Accounts from the Tools menu.

2. Click the Groups tab and then click New. Create a group called *Clerks* with a Personal ID of *Cashiers*, and click OK.

   Having created the Clerks group, let's add a couple of user accounts to it. Here are the steps:

1. Click the Users tab and then click New. In the New User/-Group dialog box, type *Joe Cash* under both Name and Personal ID and then click OK.

2. Add Joe Cash to the Clerks group by selecting Clerks in the Available Groups list and clicking the Add button.

Importing databases

Access 97 can import databases created by many other programs. Simply choose Get External Data and then Import from the File menu, select a format, locate the database file, and click Import. Depending on the format you've selected, Access may use a wizard to obtain the additional information it needs to convert and display the file.

3. Repeat steps 1 and 2 to add a user called *Dolly Bills* to the Clerks group and then click OK.

We now have a new group with two user accounts assigned to it. Next we need to tell Access what types of activities these users can perform. Follow these steps to set the permissions for the new Clerks group:

1. Choose Security and then User And Group Permissions from the Tools menu to display the User And Group Permissions dialog box.

Assigning group permissions

2. To display a list of existing groups, click the Groups option in the User/Group Name list box, and then select Clerks.

3. With Table selected as the Object Type, select Rentals in the Object Name list, click the Read Data, Update Data, and Insert Data check boxes in the Permissions section, and click Apply.

4. Because the Rentals table is related to the Customers, Movies, Terms, and Videos tables, select each of them in turn and assign the Read Data permission.

5. Change the Object Type to Form, select Rentals in the Object Name list, click the Open/Run check box, and click Apply.

Members of the Clerks group can now work with the Rentals table and the corresponding form. But suppose Joe Cash is also allowed to open new customer accounts. Here's how to give him permissions that the rest of his group doesn't have:

1. In the User And Group Permissions dialog box, click the Users option and select Joe Cash from the User/Group Name list box.

Assigning user permissions

2. Change the Object Type to Table, select Customers, click the Read Data, Update Data, and Insert Data check boxes, and then click Apply.

3. Change the Object Type to Form, select New Customers, click the Open/Run check box, click Apply, and then click OK to close the dialog box.

Now follow these steps to test the new group's security:

Testing security

1. Quit Access, and then restart the program, logging on as *Dolly Bills* with no password. Then open the Secure Brock Buster's Video database.

2. Click the Forms tab, open the Rentals form, and then close it.

3. Now try to open the New Customers form. Because Dolly Bills doesn't have permission to work with this form, Access displays this dialog box:

The permissions for the Clerks group are obviously in effect, controlling the Access activities of this group of users.

4. Click OK to close the dialog box.

5. Quit Access, restart the program, log on as *Joe Cash* (no password), open the Secure Brock Buster's Video database, and test this user's permissions.

With that brief demonstration, we'll leave you to explore database security on your own.

Removing Security Settings

Before we end this chapter, we'll show you how to undo the security measures we've put in place. Follow these steps:

1. Quit and restart Access, logging on as *Owner*, and then open the Secure Brock Buster's Video database.

2. Choose Security and then User And Group Accounts from the Tools menu.

The User-Level Security Wizard

In order for you to better understand the process for creating a secure database, we have taken you through all the steps manually. However, once you have a good grasp of database security, you may want to explore the User-Level Security Wizard. To create a secure database using the wizard, first complete the four bulleted steps listed on page 153. Then choose Security and User-Level Security Wizard from the Tools menu to activate the wizard. When you complete the wizard's dialog boxes, Access takes care of the fifth and sixth bulleted steps. Access also encrypts the database. You then need to complete the final bulleted step as usual.

3. On the Users tab, delete Joe Cash and Dolly Bills by selecting them from the Name list and clicking the Delete button. Then add Admin to the Admins group and click Clear Password.

Deleting users

4. On the Groups tab, delete the Clerks group. Then click OK to close the dialog box.

Deleting groups

5. Choose Security and then User And Group Permissions from the Tools menu.

6. Click the Change Owner tab, make sure that Admin appears in the New Owner edit box, and then for each Object Type except Database, select all the items in the Object list and click Change Owner. (To select all the items together, click the first item, hold down the Shift key, and click the last item on the list.)

Changing the database owner

7. Click the Permissions tab and select Admin in the User/Group Name list box. For each Object Type, select all the items in the Object Name list and click the Administer check box twice to ensure that full permissions are assigned to the Admin user. Then click Apply. When you are finished, click OK.

Assigning full permissions

8. Quit Access and restart the program. Because the Admins group now includes an Admin user with no password, Access automatically logs you into the program as that user. (Now you can see why the first security measure was to create a new Admins user and remove the Admin user from that group!)

9. Open the Secure Brock Buster's Video database and then choose Security and Users And Group Accounts from the Tools menu. Delete the Owner user and click OK.

Congratulations! You have completed your Quick Course in Access. By now, you should feel comfortable with all the components of Access, in spite of the complexity of the program and of databases in general. With the basics you have learned here, together with the Help feature and the sample databases that come with the program, you should be able to tackle the creation of some pretty sophisticated databases. Good luck!

Index

Other *Quick Course®* books

Don't miss the other titles in our *Quick Course®* series! Quality books at an unbeatable price.

Quick Course® in Windows 95
Quick Course® in Microsoft Office 97
Quick Course® in Word 97
Quick Course® in Excel 97
Quick Course® in PowerPoint 97
Quick Course® in the Internet using Netscape Navigator, Versions 2 & 3
Quick Course® in Microsoft Office for Windows 95 and Windows NT
Quick Course® in Access 7 for Windows 95
Quick Course® in Word 7 for Windows 95
Quick Course® in Excel 7 for Windows 95
Quick Course® in Microsoft Office 4.3 for Windows
Quick Course® in Access 2 for Windows
Quick Course® in Word 6 for Windows
Quick Course® in Excel 5 for Windows
Quick Course® in PowerPoint 4 for Windows
Quick Course® in Microsoft Works 3 for Windows
Quick Course® in WordPerfect 6.1 for Windows
Quick Course® in Lotus 1-2-3 Release 4 for Windows
Quick Course® in Windows 3.1
Quick Course® in Windows for Workgroups

Plus more!

For a copy of our latest catalog, call (800) 854-3344, fax (206) 641-4728, send email to onlinepressinc@msn.com, or write to the following address:

Online Press Inc.
14320 NE 21st Street, Suite 18
Bellevue, WA 98007

You can also browse our catalog online by visiting our Web site at http://www.quickcourse.com.